FINGERPRINTS *of* God

SURVIVING AN OPIOID CRISIS

C.S. TRENARY

Fingerprints of God: Surviving an Opioid Crisis

FingerprintsOfGodBook@gmail.com

Printed in the United States of America

Design: Carla Green, Clarity Designworks

ISBN paperback 978-0-57858014-2

This book is dedicated to my two precious boys,
who have been my inspiration. Many times, I wanted to give up
and crawl into a corner but your tender sweetness kept me going.
You gave me the drive to push forward for the sake of our family.
You are the reason I fell deeper in love with our Lord and Savior.
He became my anchor so I could hold you two up.
Thank you for being my precious sons!

Contents

Acknowledgments

I owe a debt of love to those who allowed me to share their insights about the grace and power of God in this book. In loving memory of my mother, Evelyn Stafford, who faithfully prayed for her grandsons and me. To my dear friends, Lisa Leblanc and Lisa Scott who never left my side, who always held me up, unselfishly gave of their time, and met my family's needs in so many ways. You cared enough to listen for many hours. To the Lewis family, who became an incredible source of support. To Ralph Trenary, my wonderful husband and best friend, thank you for doing life deeply with me. You are my rock! And, to so many more of you who have been true friends, you are heroes to me!

Preface

I am writing this book to encourage others in my position. The three years following my separation and divorce were some of my darkest hours; through this difficulty, God's Fingerprints have been gracefully dotted in the most perfect places. There's a verse in the Bible that I often referred to during this time, which tells God's children He will not give us more than we can handle. I am living proof that this is true. Please read my story and look for God's Fingerprints written all over it.

CHAPTER 1

In the Beginning

"I cried out to God for help; I cried out to God to hear me."

— Psalm 77:1

This ordeal began on Labor Day weekend in 1994. My husband, Jeff, and I had been married for eight wonderful years and we had so many plans, hopes and dreams for our future. Our son, Thomas—just twenty-two months old at the time—was our heart. We had spent a weekend with family at Toledo Bend reservoir in Texas. It's a beautiful part of the country that is considered by many fisherman's paradise. Jeff and I had decided to head home to Tyler, Texas a day early so we could spend a quiet Labor Day unpacking and unwinding from our weekend before returning to work on Tuesday. It was a beautiful and still Sunday afternoon. Not a cloud hanging in the sky. I can remember waving goodbye to family as we turned onto the highway leaving the campground. Little did I know, our lives were about to change forever. I rarely took the opportunity to sleep on road trips because I always felt the need to be a "passenger" driver! But this trip, I was sleepy and reluctantly fell asleep within minutes.

The next thing I remember is waking up as my body thrust forward as our brakes let out a deafening roar. Jeff was crying out, "Oh My God!" and as I gained my composure and looked up, there was a dark blue Toyota barreling out of control towards us. We were about to have everyone's worst nightmare come true, a head-on collision at a high rate of speed. It's true what they say; your life does flash before your eyes. It happened in a matter of seconds, in slow motion, my precious family's faces appeared before me, with the thought of my baby, sleeping peacefully in the back seat. I remember the moment I braced for impact.

Thomas screamed at the top of his lungs—a blood-curdling scream like I had never heard before or have never heard since to this day. I wanted so desperately to scoop him up in my arms but I couldn't. I was helpless. Jeff and I were both trapped in our seats and were unable to move due to the severity of our injuries. It seemed as though all of my ribs were broken. When I attempted to lean forward and tend to Thomas, my rib cage felt like an accordion. I thought to myself… Oh My God, this has to be a bad nightmare. Stuff like this happens to other people, not my family. All I could do was reach down and stroke Thomas' leg with my hand and tell him over and over that Mommie loved him. I was trying so hard not to panic. I didn't want Thomas to be afraid.

We were about to have everyone's worst nightmare come true, a head-on collision at a high rate of speed. It's true what they say; your life does flash before your eyes.

Meanwhile, Jeff was fading in and out of consciousness. His right knee had been shattered and he was experiencing major shock. I remember glancing down at his knee seeing his kneecap crumbled into what seemed like a million pieces. It made me literally sick to my stomach. I told myself to never look at his knee again, and I didn't. We held hands and kept repeating, "I love you." Every now and then, one of us would squeeze the other's hand. As time passed, I remember the paramedics drilling Jeff with simple questions: What is your name? Where were you born? How old are you? I knew exactly what was going on. The paramedics thought they were losing Jeff and were trying to keep him conscious. They didn't have a clue if we had internal injuries or not. Soon, Jeff stopped squeezing my hand; I thought I was watching my husband die before my very eyes. I remember screaming so loudly inside of my head until it hurt pleading with God not to take him. I couldn't imagine life without him.

The crash happened quickly, but being trapped in a mangled car seemed to last an eternity. In reality, we were probably trapped for about an hour and a half. I remember seeing a sea of red as I glanced around our car; lights flashed everywhere from numerous state trooper cars, ambulances, fire trucks. The first people on the scene stayed with us the entire time. They were an older couple who were involved in our accident but without contact. They were in the vehicle that was being passed by the teenagers who hit us. Since our car was so badly crumpled, the only thing that would open were our windows and the back doors. Looking back, this couple was very smart in asking our permission to take Thomas out of our car and bring him into their air-conditioned vehicle. There was such a stench in the air of burned rubber, pavement, oil, and gas. I later found out the firemen were extremely worried our car might ignite into flames since we had a full tank of gas. Thankfully, God protected us from an explosion or even knowing that information.

This kind lady came back to me immediately to give me a full report on Thomas and to let me know he was Ok. She held my hand tightly and stroked my forehead over and over. At times, she would rub my shoulders. It was so obvious she could sense my fear. My instinct told me she was a mother feeling my pain of being helpless. Nevertheless, she was very comforting to me. I only wish I would have known her name to thank her later.

Finally, after what seemed like hours upon hours, the "jaws of life" arrived. It made the loudest, most deafening noise, like a jack-hammer. I could not understand what was taking so long to get us out of our mangled car, having no idea what our car looked like on the outside. It seemed to take the first responders forever to cut us out. Then, suddenly, we were finally free! But I was temporarily paralyzed and could not move. I sensed the fear of the paramedic working on me. He knew my ribs were broken, among other bones, but I desperately needed oxygen to breathe. I overheard one of the paramedics say that my skin color was turning blue—a sign that my body was being deprived of oxygen. They wrapped this heavy-duty body cage around me and hoisted me sideways out of the car. This is where I cannot begin to describe in words the excruciating pain I was in. Yeah, I would say broken ribs were a very close comparison to child labor! Only, labor contractions end. My pain grew worse as they pulled me out of the wreckage.

Three hospitals later, Jeff and I both had emergency surgeries. The last hospital was in our hometown of Tyler, Texas. Tyler had a trauma hospital that was much better equipped to handle our critical injuries. Looking back, I am so thankful my great Uncle Pete and Aunt Mary drove to the Lufkin hospital (hospital #2) to check on us. They were so near and dear to our family. Uncle Pete and Aunt Mary lived only a few streets over from us in Tyler. It was so nice to have family near us, especially since our immediate families lived out of state. We actually felt like their adopted children. They would dote on Thomas whenever they had the opportunity. Uncle Pete was a retired surgeon and just didn't feel comfortable with my critical condition needing emergency surgery in a small hospital. After a second CAT scan, the results revealed that I had internal bleeding and needed immediate surgery. It was determined that I was stable enough to be transported to the Tyler hospital to have emergency surgery. Plus, Uncle Pete knew many of the practicing surgeons back home in Tyler. He just felt more comfortable with Jeff and I being in East Texas Medical Center.

By the time Jeff and I had arrived by ambulance at East Texas Medical Center, it was close to midnight. It had been over 24 hours since our accident and I had lost a lot of blood. My internal bleeding was reaching a critical point. The attending surgeon greeted us and wanted my consent to begin surgery.

Dr. Fernandez began to describe how he was going to cut me open to stop the bleeding. He believed my bleeding was coming from my spleen, which had been lacerated by my broken ribs and determined that it would be fatal if I didn't have the surgery now. All I could think of was how big my incision was going to be. Two years earlier, I would give birth to Thomas via C-section. In reality, a C-section incision is not big but I remember the recovery process being rather painful. So, while I was lying on this stretcher with multiple broken bones, my attention was now on the size of the incision this surgeon would make on me. The surgeon appeared to be a little inpatient with me for hesitating to sign the consent form. Instead, I asked him how large my incision would be? He held up his two hands about a foot apart and said probably twelve inches. My heart sunk and I began to panic in my mind until I heard the nurse tell the doctor that my blood pressure was dropping to 55 over 30. I was still coherent enough to know that my blood pressure was dangerous and I was going to die if I didn't have surgery immediately.

Surgery lasted a few hours into the early morning. I had lost a lot of blood and needed a transfusion during surgery. I flat-lined once on the operating table, but by the grace of God, Dr. Fernandez was able to perform a successful surgery!

When I awoke in recovery, I felt my hands being held tightly by my mother and brother. My brother had driven my mother up from Louisiana during the night to the hospital in Tyler. When I opened my eyes, they were both smiling and said I was going to be just fine. I could not say anything because I was on a respirator. They kept squeezing my hands, reassuring me, reminding me to stay calm. It was rather overwhelming the first time I opened my eyes to see monitors on both sides of my bed, along with what seemed like a gazillion tubes coming out of me. I couldn't move or talk but only lay there. Time stood still.

Jeff and I were in intensive care for several days following our surgeries. Our hospital rooms were flooded with visitors' every day. During this time, I felt an incredible amount of love. I truly never dreamed that so many people cared about us. Friends really took time out of their day to come see us in the hospital. I was very grateful. You know they say that God can bring good out of every tragedy or mishap. In fact, there's a verse in Romans 8:28 (*And we know that in all things God works for the good of those who love him, who have been called according to his purpose*) that addresses this very issue. What the enemy meant for harm, God can turn into something good. This happened to be true in our case.

Weeks before our accident, we had joined a new church, Southern Oaks Baptist Church. When our Youth Minister and his wife learned of our accident, they immediately rushed down to Lufkin (second hospital) to check on us. It was in Lufkin that it was determined I needed emergency surgery to stop internal bleeding. Alicia and Trey were like glue to us the whole time we were hospitalized. They held my hand tightly as the surgeon described in detail the exploratory surgery I was about to undergo. To be quite honest, I was terrified. With Jeff on the gurney next to me—basically helpless and out of it, medicated with drugs—and my mother and brother on their way from Louisiana, Alicia, Trey, Uncle Pete, and Aunt Mary were it. For that moment, they were life-line, my family and my comfort.

Alicia and Trey came to visit us daily at the hospital. It felt like we had been forever friends. A relationship of best friends was born the week of our hospitalization. I can definitely say without a shadow of doubt, getting a true best friend out of this deal was one of the best things God brought out of our crash. (Again, let me refer you to Romans 8:28.) We remained close best friends and sisters for years following the accident.

She was the sister I never had and I could tell her anything without fear of judgment. Friends like Alicia are a rare treasure from God. Please note here, you have just read one of my first Fingerprints from God in this trial!

Needless to say, surviving a near fatal head-on collision was an awakening in my life. Things were put into perspective and pretty much have been ever since. Not many of us have the experience of kissing death in the face and getting a second chance at life.

CHAPTER 2

After the Crash

"Therefore, as we have the opportunity, let us do good to all people, especially to those who belong to the family of believers."

—Galatians 6:10

As I mentioned in Chapter 1, our family had just joined Southern Oaks Baptist Church, a multi-generational church in our neighborhood. It felt like home the moment we walked through the doors. Everyone was so warm and friendly; many church members stopped by our home to say hello and welcome us. One older member even brought us a warm baked apple pie and ice cream! We were excited about our decision to join Southern Oaks and looking forward to getting to know our new friends. Our youth minister, Trey, had stopped in one evening, to visit and see if we wanted to get more involved by teaching Sunday School to high school juniors and seniors. He said it would be a great way to get to know other church members and really connect. Honestly, I thought he was crazy. We had never worked with youth before in our lives. We were practically kids ourselves. What could we possibly offer?

It felt like home the moment we walked through the doors.

I didn't think I was cut out for the challenge! However, Jeff reminded me that the only way to really get to know people was to do life deeply with them by serving at church. We really didn't have many friends in Tyler since we had recently moved there. It was time to start planting roots.

The moment we arrived home from the hospital, our new church family rolled up their sleeves to help. In fact, due to our injuries, we needed help for a good six to eight weeks taking care of Thomas and ourselves. Jeff had a long cast on his right leg and I had one on my left leg. We were a pair on crutches! Plus, we were also recovering from our surgeries and broken ribs. Getting around in our home was initially difficult to say the least. Taking care of Thomas was a challenge. He was almost two years old and very active, like any other toddler his age. I was so thankful my mother was able to stay a few weeks to help us get back on our feet.

The parents of these high school students we taught in Sunday school were amazing! They orchestrated everything from delivering home-cooked meals, babysitting Thomas and taking care of our lawn for weeks. We were blessed beyond measure. Another family went out of their way and spent a lot of time investing in us. David and Natalie Hudson and their three children had recently moved to Tyler and joined Southern Oaks about the time we joined, so we already had a lot in common with them, being new in town ourselves. We taught their two older kids in Sunday school. Our relationship with the Hudson family deepened over the next three years; they became like family to us. Jeff and David became accountability partners. Their older kids were always hanging out at our home. Looking back, you can connect the dots and see God's Fingerprints all over this. He strategically planted us at Southern Oaks ahead of the crash so our new church family would be in place to minister to us afterwards. Also, God strategically used Trey to introduce us to all of these wonderful high school parents. Imagine what blessings we could have missed out on if we weren't willing to serve?

Jeff's injuries were evident more as time passed on. In the years following the accident, he had additional surgeries; two knee surgeries and two back surgeries. Describing those years would require another book, but I will say that these were difficult years, having to watch him suffer so much. Before his last back surgery, he had been told by numerous surgeons that he should not be experiencing the degree of pain he was having. *BUT*, they offered, here's some painkillers in the meantime. To make a long story short, he had to have fusion surgery, during which a titanium cage was inserted into his back. By the time this surgery was performed, it was too late; he was addicted to prescription painkillers. His injuries and lack of proper diagnosis gave birth to Jeff's opioid crisis.

I need to insert a very important fact here. Prior to Jeff's major back surgery, we welcomed our second son into this world, Drew. I never dreamed I could love a second child so much. As many parents know, when you have your first child, the whole world revolves around them! It's hard to imagine loving another human being so much. So, when the second one arrives, you wonder if you have enough within your inner being to love another child as much. It's amazing how thoroughly God wired humans with the capacity to love. It was love at first sight when I saw Drew!

Now back to the story. I did not suspect an opioid addiction until 1999, five years after our wreck. At this time, we had been living in Oklahoma. With David's help, our family was able to relocate to Tulsa, where he had been offered a great opportunity with an international construction firm firm in Tulsa. The Hudson family had moved up a few months earlier and we were so excited to be near this precious family again. In January of 1998, Jeff had accepted a job at the same company where David worked. It was a great opportunity for our family as well. Jeff was being groomed for a vice president position and, best of all, Jeff and David were able to work together. Jeff had the world in his hands with such a promising career ahead of him. Please take special note, another Fingerprint toward God's divine intervention. Crossing paths with the Hudson family those years earlier was not a coincidence.

The opioid addiction was continuing to grow in silence. A year later, Jeff admitted to our pastor, David, and me, that he became addicted to prescription painkillers following our car wreck. This addiction had been his secret for five years. I was heartbroken. I was devastated. How could he have hidden such a secret from me? Well, I've learned through the years that an addict can be very clever even to his family. Usually, an addict doesn't know he or she is an addict. Jeff's confession was full of grace. He was going to overcome this addiction through the help of God, family, and friends. The next Sunday, he stood up and gave his testimony and confession to our Sunday school class. At this time, I felt pretty confident that everything was going to be OK. The addiction would be behind us. Was this perhaps naïve thinking on my part?

Life had been great until the winter of 2000 when Jeff's company merged with another sister company from California. It brought on tremendous stress for the office. It also created extra work hours and more deadlines, without additional staffing in Jeff's software department. This stress began to bring on the monster of his addiction. It was starting to come out of the closet again without any of us suspecting it. We were blinded initially. Remember, Satan is the master of disguise. We must keep our armor on at all times and be on guard from attacks—whether that entails work-stress or the stresses of life in general.

During this time, Jeff was being lured away from his promising career, being enticed to begin a brand new career selling life insurance. More autonomy. More independence. More opportunity. No accountability. Everything sounded wonderful—to Jeff. But I was dying inside and caving into fear since Jeff had never sold a thing in his life. It just didn't feel right but I was trusting in my husband of fourteen years to make the right decision. He claimed he had spent time with the Lord on this decision and so I had to trust him as his wife.

Being in sales is a tough career but success can be achieved through hard work and determination. Though, having thick skin is probably the strongest characteristic a person should have to push forward. Ninety percent of your business is met with rejection and the remaining ten percent can make or break you. It only takes a few good sales to gain financial success. However, a huge dose of rejection and an addiction doesn't mix well.

I'm not going to lie—waiting on the Lord is tough, but He is always faithful to those who wait upon him patiently. Faith is unseen.

Hindsight is 20/20. If only we could have a taste of the future. So many costly and painful mistakes would not be made. This is when as believers we need to put our trust in the Lord. Seek Him daily on every decision and He will be a guiding light. This reminds me of a verse I recently memorized to remind me of this promise: *Whether you turn to the right or to the left, your ears will hear a voice behind you saying this is the way; walk in it* (Isaiah 30:21). Too many of us get caught up in the moment and want a quick fix for everything. I've had my moments of being guilty of this. We live in a disposable society. If we don't like the food at one drive-thru restaurant, then we go to the next restaurant until we're satisfied. I'm not going to lie—waiting on the Lord is tough, but He is always faithful to those who wait upon Him patiently. Faith is unseen.

CHAPTER 3

Life Unraveling

"We must pay the most careful attention, therefore, to what we have heard, so that we do not drift away."
— Hebrews 2:1

Against the advice and wisdom of many, Jeff left his promising career of becoming vice president of an international firm within a year in exchange for becoming an insurance sales agent. David was disappointed his friend had chosen another path that didn't make sense.

The first six months of Jeff's new career was a mirror image to that of a model rookie. In fact, he was the number one new agent in the Tulsa area during his first six months with Horizon Life. But things started happening that just didn't make much sense. Or, let's just say there were too many mishaps going on.

While Jeff's career seemed to be taking off, my mother was hospitalized for a week during Easter break with a low sodium count. It was then determined that other things were going on with my mother. She couldn't shake this low-grade fever that lasted for about three months. As soon as the boys' school was out for the summer, I had made arrangements for the three of us to fly down to Louisiana for a few days leaving Dad at home to work. I wanted to check on my mother and give Thomas and Drew the opportunity to visit family and have some cousin time.

I can remember the phone call. I had been packing our suitcases all afternoon for our trip to Louisiana the next day. It was Jeff on the other end. He said he just wanted to let me know that he was OK. I said OK, would you like to elaborate? He went on to explain that he had been involved in an accident in which he had hit a tree and flipped his car. He was calling from the emergency room. Needless to say, I freaked out. I quickly delegated my boys over to neighbors so I could rush to the hospital and be with Jeff. Thankfully, his injuries were minor but his accident caused me to cancel our trip home to Louisiana.

The next month, I somehow found a way to get down to Louisiana in time for Mom's exploratory surgery. Her fever persisted which began to bring on the concern that something else was happening with her health.

This time around, I went home without my kids. It was the first time I had traveled eight hours in a car alone. That is a lot of windshield time to be alone but weirdly, I loved it. It gave me time to be still. I turned off the radio. As my Mother would say, you can really get to know yourself with that much time on your hands. I decided to spend my time talking with God. With my crazy busy "Mom" schedule, I had lacked a great deal of time with Him. Being a stay-at-home Mom is by far the greatest job in the world but your duties of multi-tasking are endless. I was always being pulled in a million directions and it seemed I never had much time for God or even myself. This is mistake number one, which I've learned the hard way over and over. God deserves your best rather than your left-over time. It never fails—when I seem to be having a rotten week or there is major chaos in my day, I realize that I have not spent time being still with Him. That is often the way my Father gets my attention. I am so thankful that we serve a God who constantly gives us do-overs.

It never fails—when I seem to be having a rotten week or there is major chaos in my day, I realize that I have not spent time being still with Him. That is often the way my Father gets my attention.

Over the last few years, a neighbor and I would meet weekly to lift up our families in prayer. However, with summer in full swing and kids home, our opportunities to meet for prayer dwindled down to hardly ever. Amazingly, I looked forward to the long drive home to Louisiana.

Practically my entire trip consisted of dialogue between God and me. A great deal of the time I did way too much talking. Though, we do worship a mighty and powerful God who has a deep sense of humor. I have spent many hours laughing with Him. I am thankful He has patience with me and always listens to me no matter what the circumstances. I often find myself in awe that the master and creator of our vast universe has time for me and my little problems. By the time I made it to Alexandria eight hours later, God had given me a priceless treasure. He gave me this incredible, unsurpassable peace that Mom was going to be just fine. I tell you the truth, this feeling was unshakeable. Please note, you have just read another Fingerprint from God.

During my Mom's exploratory surgery, it was determined that she had Hodgkin's Lymphoma. This was a form of cancer. I thought to myself, not again! God, not again, *please*. My father died of cancer eleven years earlier. I wasn't ready to lose my Mom. Cancer has been an enemy in our family. Within four years, cancer had claimed the lives of my dad, grandmother and aunt. I hated the word cancer!

As my Mother's doctor began to share the news with our family, everyone became upset except me. You may ask what was wrong with me? A loved one being diagnosed with cancer is devastating. Deep down in the core of my soul, God had given me the peace that Mom would be OK. Up until then, there had been very few times in my life that I truly felt 100% peace without a shadow of doubt. I hung onto that peace tighter than ever. We were elated to learn that Hodgkin's Lymphoma is the most treatable cancer with a cure rate as high as 90 percent. At the time of writing of this book, Mom has been in remission for over eleven years. Praise God! Please note here, a mega Fingerprint from God! In fact, my boys thanked God for years in their nightly prayers for taking away Grandma's cancer.

Meanwhile, Jeff's short-lived reign as the top-producing agent was beginning to crumble. He went months without selling a policy. He was beginning to dip into our hard-earned savings without much blessing from me. However, I had faith in him and had to trust him as my husband that he would turn things around. Jeff had always excelled at whatever he set his mind to do. Little did I know the real reason for his lack of sales? The enemy had been invited in and was beginning to show his face without any of us knowing it. We should always be alert. The only way the enemy has a key into our lives is when we invite him in through words, actions, television, movies, you name it. An addiction to drugs or alcohol, a premarital or extramarital affair—even something as simple as the music we listen to can give the enemy a foothold in our lives. We must have the armor of Christ on at all times.

CHAPTER 4

My Turn

"So do not fear, for I am with you; do not be dismayed, for I am your God. I will strengthen you and help you; I will uphold you with my righteous right hand."

— Isaiah 41:10

It was then July 2001, and we were in the hottest part of Oklahoma's steamy summers. In Tulsa, our temperatures would easily climb to 100-plus degrees for days and weeks at a time. Daydreaming about winter during this time was not uncommon for me! Freezing my tail off didn't seem like such a bad idea in the middle of those heat waves.

Thomas was in the middle of summer baseball. Aside from complaints about the heat, this was a time in our lives that I cherished. Kids and summer baseball, what more could I want? I lived for this stuff.

I can clearly remember the moment I started feeling ill, sitting at one of Thomas' games. It was like fog rolling onto shore, but moving over my body in slow motion. I started feeling groggy and tired. When we got home from his game later that night, I took my temperature and discovered I had a low-grade fever. Crud, I was getting sick in the summer. I didn't have *time* to be sick. The next week, my fever persisted. So, I figured it was now time to visit a doctor. My doctor couldn't exactly pinpoint what was wrong but prescribed a round of antibiotics. A week later, my low-grade fever continued to linger. Again, another trip to the doctor. This time, he ran more tests and thought I had signs of a bladder infection. Here we go again, another round of antibiotics. A week later, my fever was still hanging around. This time, I had symptoms of chest pains so I was sent to a cardiologist. This was beginning to become a frustrating pattern. I went to doctor after doctor and had procedure after procedure. I had been running a low-grade fever for six weeks; I was beginning to grow more and more concerned about my health. Could I have cancer? Thoughts like that were starting to invade my innermost mind. After all, my family has had a history of cancer. Mom was in the middle of her chemotherapy treatments. I was upset that I was still sick in August because I had wanted to make another trip down to Louisiana to help her before school started for the boys. However, I could not afford to take the risk of being around her, since her immune system was in a weakened state from the chemotherapy.

School had started and I was still sick. It had been two long months of running a fever and God now had my undivided attention. I was beginning to fall to my knees pleading with God to heal me. I could have overdosed on Tylenol or Motrin and absolutely nothing would bring my fever down. What in the heck was causing my fever? I kept telling God that I couldn't be sick; my boys needed their mother to be well. During this time, I became a pincushion going to specialist after specialist. Each one ordered mega blood work. This was not a good thing for somebody who didn't like needles and blood! I underwent every imaginable procedure under the sun. If it could be scoped, it was scoped! If it could be prodded, it was prodded.

Meanwhile, Jeff had not had a sale since June and our money was beginning to dwindle. What on earth were we going to do? I didn't have the energy to work outside of our home because of my ongoing fever. Every night, I found myself going upstairs to our guest bedroom and shutting the door. Our guest room soon became my refuge. I just wanted to be alone with God. I would cry out to my Father, begging Him to take my fever away. I found every scripture in the Bible that related to sickness and healing and claimed those scriptures. I thought if I spent enough time on my knees with God, crying out scripture, that would work. Still, nothing happened. My fever persisted. I began to realize that God was fully in control and perhaps He was trying to teach me a thing or two about character and perseverance. The problem was definitely me. God is always in control.

As believers, we know this, but there are times God gives us valuable and painful life lessons to instill these realizations. Sometimes, pain is the only way He can get our attention. By the fourth month, I gave up. I told God for the first time in my life that He could have all of me. I would give Him 100% of Candy. Well, believe it or not, by the fifth month, I still had a fever and was still undergoing many more procedures. I was beginning to wonder, God, what happened? I gave you 100% last month. Ok, you can heal me now and let's move on. I kept telling Him, this time when the going got good, I would not leave Him. It's not uncommon to reach out to God during a time of crisis and when things calm down, we don't necessarily need Him as much. At least that was the case for me.

I thought if I spent enough time on my knees with God, crying out scripture, that would work. Still, nothing happened. My fever persisted. I began to realize that God was fully in control and perhaps He was trying to teach me a thing or two about character and perseverance.

Well, during this ordeal, God began knitting my life together with dear friends who would become my anchor in the years to follow. I use to think things couldn't possibly get worse with my mom having cancer, my husband's career and our finances unraveling, and my health in poor condition running fever for six straight months. Continue reading on; believe it or not but it does get worse. My story is about to become a real adventure of painful trials and tribulations. And God held me up every step of the way. He gave me the strength to stand on mountains. He gave me the strength to walk on stormy seas. He has given me His promise to never leave me nor forsake me, by showing me beautiful sunsets. I will tell you later what beautiful sunsets mean to me.

CHAPTER 5

The Admission of the Addiction

"My sins, O God, are not hidden from you; you know how foolish I have been".

— Psalm 69:5

It was January 2002. Christmas had come and gone. My fever was still there; an un-welcomed guest in my life. Jeff hadn't made a good sale since June. He was very withdrawn at home. I started thinking about his behavior and noticed a real pattern since the fall, especially on weekends. Most weekends, he would either sleep or complain of headaches. I remember I had suggested to Jeff that we should probably start praying about him changing careers and for him to consider going back into construction. He wouldn't hear of it but I asked him to please consider my request. I've always believed in supporting and holding each other up.

I would question Jeff if he had been using painkillers (opioids). He would immediately become defensive and make me feel as though I was crazy for bringing up such an accusation.

Over the last few months when things just didn't seem to add up, I would question Jeff if he had been using painkillers (opioids). He would immediately become defensive and make me feel as though I was crazy for bringing up such an accusation. Nevertheless, I started having my concerns.

I remember once again falling on my knees pleading with God for help. This time, I was determined to relentlessly continue questioning Jeff until I got an answer. Eventually, I got my answer; he finally admitted that he had been doing drugs, prescription painkillers, since September 11th. He claimed that the events of 9/11 brought on depression thus sending him to drugs. I bought it! It was a great excuse at the time. I have since learned that addicts are the cleverest actors and can convince you to believe anything. If you know of someone who may be using drugs or alcohol, please keep your antennae up. They can be clever and manipulators without even knowing it themselves. That is just how powerful an addiction can be. It's a stronghold like no other force.

With Jeff's admission of drug use, everything began to add up thus becoming crystal-clear. Of course, his sales career was in the toilet. He had allowed the enemy in much more than I had ever imagined. It would be almost a year later until I would learn the entire truth, or at least most of the truth. That night, I couldn't run up our stairs fast enough. I literally fell apart in what was now my prayer closet, our guest room. What on earth now, God? I was so angry I could spit nails. What was wrong with this picture? I found myself drawing closer to our Father. And it appeared Jeff was trying his hardest to move away from our Father. God allowed me to have my pity party and allowed me to cry my eyes out. Then, He graciously picked me up into His mighty arms, wiped my tears away and told me to trust Him: I have you in the palm of my hand and I will not let you go.

The next morning I told Jeff it was time for professional help. To date, nothing was helping him overcome his addiction. I suggested meeting with our pastor for counseling. Perhaps our pastor could guide us in the right direction or path. Thankfully, Jeff agreed.

Meanwhile, I was scheduled to have outpatient surgery that week. Didn't I have enough on my plate? Let's not forget, my fever was still there eight months later. At this time, my infectious disease doctor believed that I might have the rare disease of giant cell arteritis. This disease, typically affecting older women, causes temporal arteries to enlarge, possibly leading to blindness or even death. The only cure for this disease is taking large doses of steroids for 6-24 months. The thought of taking steroids for that long of a period terrified me, to say the least. My doctor wanted to go in and take a biopsy of my temporal artery to confirm my diagnosis before proceeding with heavy drugs.

After my surgery, I was sent home with painkillers to help ease my pain of the biopsy. I found myself hiding the painkillers from Jeff so that he would not be tempted. Thankfully, I only needed a few pills to get through my recovery. Two weeks later, when I went to find my hidden pills to throw the rest away, I discovered Jeff had already taken them! I was furious. Then, I remembered my infectious disease doctor had given me painkillers in the fall for pain I was having then. I quickly rummaged through my lingerie drawer where I had hidden those pills. I couldn't find them anywhere. I turned all of my drawers upside down and still, nothing. I couldn't believe my husband was taking my painkillers. I then called the pharmacy to see if the refill had been filled and, to my discovery, it had been refilled back in November. I remember thinking to myself, Oh my God, this problem is bigger than all of us. I didn't know what to do. Nothing seemed to be working. And in reality, the real problem was Jeff. He wasn't ready for help, which prolonged the agony for our family. The only thing I knew to do at the moment was to call our pastor for help. However, he was not available to meet with us until the next week. I thought, God you have got to help us now.

In the meantime, I got the results from my surgery, which came back negative. I was thankful for the good report, but the good report didn't answer the million-dollar question: Why did I still have fever? My doctor told me that there are often false-negatives with this type of procedure. I thought, good grief, why in the heck did I have this procedure in the first place? He felt certain that I had too many symptoms of this disease and started me on steroids anyway. Within a week of taking the steroids, I felt wonderful. I felt normal again. However, I was reminded that this temporary high was strictly drug-induced as a result of the steroids. Though, I did take advantage of feeling good and did some much needed and neglected house cleaning. It had been months since I had done any deep cleaning. I continued taking the steroids for three months and thankfully, I didn't suffer from any of the major side-effects attributed to steroid use. My Sunday school class was praying that I would not experience any side-effects. Please note, another Fingerprint here!

I was thankful for the good report, but the good report didn't answer the million-dollar question: Why did I still have fever?

Finally, it was time for the meeting with our pastor. This meeting could not happen soon enough for me. I was proud of Jeff for bearing his heart and soul in front of our pastor. He appeared to be genuine. He had told the pastor that the drugs had become a controlling force in his life and he needed help. Our pastor was receptive and admitted that he was no expert in the area but would look into help for Jeff. He prayed with us. I left that meeting hopeful that things would work out. Though I will say, we didn't get immediate answers. I will not blame anyone but for whatever reason, counselors did not return phone calls. It seemed as though every counselor we initially met with never followed through with things they said they were going to do on our behalf. I didn't understand why, but God did. During this time, Jeff began revealing more and more details of his addiction, which were heartbreaking, to say the least. However, give me the respect, tell me the truth and I can deal with most anything.

It was May and the end of school was quickly approaching. My boys were counting not only the days left of school but the hours, too! So much was happening this month. God gave me the biggest Fingerprint yet. In His perfect timing, He healed me of my fever. For the first time in ten months, I was fever-free! All I could say was Praise God, Praise God, Praise God! My fever left as mysteriously as it came last July. I didn't care how it left, I was well. To this day, my infectious disease doctor thought I may have had giant cell arteritis, but that my condition was still a mystery. There were so many unanswered questions.

On the financial front, our checkbook was unraveling before my eyes. Jeff never balanced our checkbook and it made me feel insecure not knowing the status of our finances. I look back and should have taken more initiative and control of the situation. I guess I hid behind the role of being a supportive and submissive wife. However, I was trying to be obedient to God.

Here's a time when Jeff revealed more about our finances. In two months and without my knowledge, both family and friends had given Jeff $9,000 to help with our living expenses, since Jeff was not bringing in any income. All of that money was gone in nearly six weeks. Honestly, I became almost hysterical as I was trying to balance our checkbook. Nothing added up. Many of the entries did not make sense. I remember that evening Jeff reluctantly walked into our bedroom. I was sitting on our bed with our laptop and bank statements scattered everywhere. He quietly sat beside me with tears in his eyes and said we needed to talk. He said he had to pay off a pharmacist for drugs he had gotten in January. This pharmacist worked for a national chain. Jeff told me he had to pay off his debt immediately because this pharmacist was making verbal threats to harm the boys and me. He knew where we lived because of the pharmacy's database. I thought to myself how much worse can this get? I really can't explain my thoughts or feelings for that evening, nor the next few weeks. I was numb. I was in shock. I felt betrayed once again. Honesty didn't appear to be an option with him.

CHAPTER 6

A Lost Job, A New Job and a Monster

"If we deliberately keep on sinning after we have received the knowledge of the truth, no sacrifice for sins is left, but only a fearful expectation of judgment and of raging fire that will consume the enemies of God"
—Hebrews 10:26-27

The time had arrived for Jeff to give up his job with Horizon Life. Too much time had passed without any results. His manager had given him a two-week notice. Jeff had never been without a job since having graduated from college; though, not producing sales wasn't much of a job either. I began calling on all of our prayer warriors hoping God would grant him a job quickly because we were almost out of money. I had learned that Jeff had cashed in many of our investment funds without my knowledge. Again, the feeling of betrayal inside of me was growing bigger and bigger. My forgiving heart was beginning to harden. But God being the sovereign God that He is gave Jeff a job two weeks later, which was unheard of at the time. Tulsa was going through a major economic slump and people were losing their jobs. God rewarded him with a job to provide for his family. Though, I truly feel in my heart the 30% pay cut was perhaps a consequence for all of his actions? God is slow to anger but He does reprimand his children for their disobedience. Habitual disobedience is something God will not allow

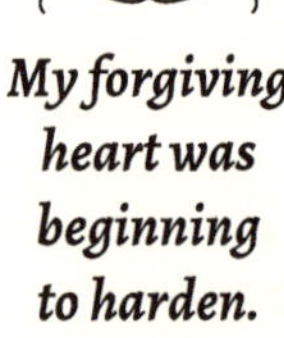

without consequences. He's very patient but He is a God of justice. He's never rewarded His children for going against His principles.

Through the fog, there were still rays of sunshine. At this time, we had a reason to celebrate. Billy Hudson, David and Natalie's oldest child, was getting married to a beautiful young lady. We had hosted Elle's Bridesmaid luncheon in our home. Jeff was so excited to help with the activities. He spent the day washing our windows. I hadn't seen that kind of "spark" in Jeff in a long time. Billy was near and dear to Jeff's heart. When we lived in Tyler, Billy would often come over to our home on the weekends and hang out with us.

The day after Billy's wedding, Jeff claimed he couldn't find his wallet. After a few days of searching, he concluded that his wallet must have been stolen out of his car. That night, I made a call to our credit card company trying to determine if any charges had been made since Friday. To my surprise, there was already $500 in cash advances made against our card. I was angry. Somehow I knew Jeff was involved but I couldn't put my finger on it. I remember I then tossed my wallet to Jeff and told him to call all of the credit card companies one by one canceling our cards. He probably spent the next two hours or more on the phone making calls. In the meantime, I was scared that his identity would be stolen. His driver's license, a family picture of us and other credit cards were in his wallet. Not only had this thief already stolen $500 from us, I thought to myself that this thief knew where we lived and what we looked like. How scary a thought! I was uneasy for at least a week—every time I saw a car that I didn't recognize drive down our street. I kept a very watchful eye on our boys. I'll admit that I was scared. We had our small group at church praying that the thief would be busted. What bothered me was that Jeff didn't appear to be too upset by the whole ordeal. What was his deal? Was he depressed, high on opioids, or did he know something?

Prayers were being answered on our behalf! The next week, the fraud unit from Visa called me with locations of the cash withdrawals made against our card. One location was at a bank in the town of Claremore, thirty minutes away from Tulsa. After getting all of the contact information, I called that bank and spoke with the manager to explain what had happened to my husband. She said they would review their videotapes for that particular day and would be able to find the frame in which the transaction was made. She promised she would call me as soon as they had a picture of the suspect. Oh, I was so relieved and felt we were making some headway. Later that evening, I couldn't wait to share the news with Jeff. When I told him, he had a puzzled look on his face. He didn't say too much the rest of the evening. What on earth was going on in his head? But around nine o'clock that evening, my life changed and the way I viewed my husband changed forever. I can remember him sitting up in bed watching TV. He turned off the TV and said we needed to talk. I said OK and continued walking around our bedroom, picking up clothes. I looked up and saw him crying his eyes out. By this time, it was really hard to embrace him or have mercy for him. I had been deceived so many countless times. He had been slowly sucking out all of the love I had for him. I still loved him but it was not the same.

He began to tell me he needed help and was a drug addict. He begged for my help and his confessions flowed out like rapid currents in a river. He asked, remember when we lived in Tyler, Texas and I accidentally drove a nail into my hand? I said yes and he admitted that he did it intentionally so he could make an emergency room visit to get drugs. I took a big deep gulp of air. My heart sank. Then he asked, do you remember my car getting torched in Tyler? He said it wasn't vandals. I began to feel myself slumping down into my chair, trying to catch my breath and breathe. He said, remember the pharmacist who threatened our family? The pharmacist didn't exist, I made up the story. I spent over $7,000 in six weeks on doctor appointments to get drugs. I thought to myself, oh my God, what kind of person am I married to who could make up such a cruel story? Who could make up a story in which there were physical threats made against his young boys? Then he asked, remember my car accident when I hit that tree on Riverside Drive? I did it on purpose so I could get drugs. Remember when my wallet was stolen? It wasn't stolen; it was me, getting cash advances for drugs. There were so many more "remember-whens" that night. I remember sitting there trembling, unable to move an inch of my body in any direction. I did not have it within me to console him as he was crying out for help. I quietly told him that I would stand by his side and we would look for other counselors. It was time for detox! Did opioids truly cause my husband to become a monster? Back then, nobody talked about opioid addictions.

I can remember I barely had the energy to change my clothes and get ready for bed. Life had truly been sucked out of me that night, along with a lot of the love I had for my husband. A huge part of my marriage died that night. My love for him was dwindling. I could barely put my feet in front of me. I had to go upstairs. I had to go in my prayer closet and spend time with God. I remember falling on my guest bed, crying for hours. I didn't sleep at all that night. What now, God? How much worse will you let it get? I'm still standing here and I haven't left your side. *Where are you, God?* Why are you hiding your face? I can't bear this pain any longer.

Did opioids truly cause my husband to become a monster? Back then, nobody talked about opioid addictions.

We didn't have the money to send Jeff to a detox hospital. He was so adamant about going to a Christian hospital. He didn't want a worldly view of detox. He even met with a pastor who was gifted in setting people free from bondage. So many demons came out of the closet during that session. It was also discovered during this session that generational sin had plagued Jeff's family for many generations. Then, for the next few months, we saw our associate pastor, Henry Townsend, for counseling regularly. Plus, Jeff attended various Christian support groups two and three times per week around town. Still, nothing worked. I was beginning to realize that Jeff didn't want to change. His heart had been so hardened. He was blinded by sin that he couldn't see the forest for the trees.

The first time we sin in a certain area of our life, we may be convicted by the Holy Spirit to stay strong and not do it again. However, if you continue to commit the same type of sin over and over, it becomes routine. It becomes habitual. Your heart begins to harden and then you begin to justify your actions. Habitual sin builds the wall higher and higher between God and you. Your fellowship in Christ is eventually broken. Nobody is immune; we are all a few steps from falling away at all times. The good news is that God wants to heal you if you let Him. It's a choice He gives you. He will never force Himself on you. He grants us free will.

It was Thanksgiving week in 2002. We had family from Louisiana visiting us for the holidays. Jeff's brother's wife and their kids from Baton Rouge along with my mother had driven up for the week. Our boys were excited to see their cousins. As they were unpacking and getting settled in, I received a phone call from the Tulsa police wanting to talk with Jeff. Apparently, their narcotics officer was investigating an incident which happened in the summer involving Jeff's car. Someone had posed as a doctor and called in a prescription for opioids. When that person arrived, the pharmacist questioned the driver and he sped away. The license plate belonged to Jeff. I thought surely this would be a wake-up call for Jeff. Jeff was then fired from his job for poor performance. The excessive use of opioids had altered his mind so much that he couldn't perform his job. Here we go again—what in the world were we going to do? I had had enough. I was nervous but I knew God was in control. I knew in my heart I had been faithful to Him and I knew He wouldn't let me down.

I knew we could get through the holidays and I had faith that Jeff could find another job. My nephew was getting married Christmas weekend in Louisiana and our younger son, Drew, was going to be the ring bearer. This was a position in which Drew needed a lot of convincing that it was a good thing. Initially, my little turkey refused to do it but with a lot of bribing and coaxing from my mother, Jeff and me, he agreed to be the ring bearer. Oh, let me quickly say, I don't believe in bribery but there are certain situations in life where you just don't have a choice! And convincing your six-year-old son to be a ring bearer in a wedding qualifies!

The excessive use of opioids had altered his mind so much that he couldn't perform his job.

It was now the week before the wedding and Christmas, and I had lots of things to accomplish before we left for Louisiana. I remember it was a Monday and Drew and I were at the bank getting stuff out of our bank box. Our account was on the banker's monitor and I noticed some discrepancies in Thomas and Drew's saving's accounts. I asked the rep to pull up those particular accounts. Thomas' account had been closed out and most of Drew's money was gone. I could feel my heart sinking as I sat there in the chair. Jeff had stolen money from his own kids' saving's accounts. I lost it. Drew and I left the bank and I began calling Jeff on his cell phone. He didn't answer but I left a message telling him it was an emergency.

An hour later, he finally returned my call. I questioned him about the accounts and he admitted that he had taken the money out a few weeks ago. I then asked him what he was doing. Instead of looking for a job, Jeff was busy trying to obtain more drugs. Jeff admitted that he just left a dentist's office and was driving around South Tulsa taking pills. He had started taking money out of our home equity. Because we had put so much down on our home purchase, we qualified and had an open-ended home equity loan available to use if we ever needed. I recently learned that, without my knowledge, he had taken out many other transactions against our home equity loan, totaling thousands of dollars. For the first time in our sixteen years of marriage, I started screaming at him. I had had enough! I could no longer handle this opioid addiction. He was causing so much harm to our family. I told him exactly what I thought. My throat literally hurt several days afterward. I was so angry, mad, hurt, and tired of the endless lies. Many wonder why I'm so sensitive to honesty. I especially get upset when family members lie. I hold them much more accountable. I told him to drive himself to the detox hospital immediately and don't leave until they admit you. We had made two earlier attempts trying to get Jeff admitted. The problem was that I was present at these two previous attempts and he didn't want to admit the extent of his drug use in front of me. I learned this information later. At this point, I didn't know what else to do. We had tried everything.

CHAPTER 7

The Death of a Marriage

"Blessed are those who have regard for the weak; the Lord delivers them in times of trouble. The Lord protects and preserves them—they are counted among the blessed in the land"

— PSALM 41:1-2A

JEFF WAS ADMITTED INTO DETOX the week before Christmas. Telling our boys that Daddy was in the hospital was probably the hardest thing I had to do. I had to be clever and watch my wording. At the same time, I didn't want to lie to my boys either. Believe me, I prayed and begged God to speak through me before confronting my boys. So, I told them their Dad was in a place that could provide him with a lot of help. They knew that their Dad had not been the same for a long time.

In the meantime, so many of our friends began to rally around us and support us in every possible way. It was so sweet and touching for me to witness such random acts of love. I was left speechless and still am today when I think about it. For instance, Jeff's men's Bible study group pulled their resources together and gave me $2,100 to help us through the holidays. My breath was taken away when it was delivered by one of his friends. Stuff like this just doesn't happen to me. Then, another dear friend dropped a $200 gift certificate to Walmart in Drew's church bag. I just didn't know exactly how to respond to that kind of kindness and generosity. Again, more Fingerprints from God! I don't particularly like giving dollar amounts but I am so you can have a perspective of what I was beginning to experience.

I was beginning to have my first true glimpses of humility. I'd never in my life been in a position where I needed this kind of support. A dear friend reminded me that humility is a characteristic of Christ. He is more interested in developing our character than anything else. She was right but nevertheless, it didn't feel comfortable. I was out of my comfort zone. In the many months ahead, God will deal with me regarding this characteristic trait of Christ. The molding and shaping will be a long journey. Though, if we truly wish to grow in Christ, then He will sometimes take us out of our nice comfort zone and use us to accomplish His purposes. We will forever be in a "construction zone" until we draw our last breath on earth.

A dear friend reminded me that humility is a characteristic of Christ. He is more interested in developing our character than anything else.

Jeff stayed in the hospital for a week; thus, making it impossible for him to make the trip down to Louisiana in time for my nephew's wedding. It was so difficult putting on a strong face in front of my family. I didn't dare put a damper on Matthew's wedding by letting them know Jeff was in detox. I would not allow our problems to rain on the biggest day of Matthew's life. Though, I shared a lot the day after the wedding. Needless to say, my family was upset.

Jeff was finally released on Sunday but refused to come to Louisiana to join his family for Christmas. He claimed he needed to be close by the hospital to attend their intensive outpatient therapy. The boys were upset and very anxious to see their Dad. It had been over a week since they set eyes on him. Two days before Christmas, Tulsa had a blizzard that blanketed the city with ten inches of snow in four hours. This dilemma created more anticipation and excitement for my boys. It was more of a difficult decision for me, but my boys agreed to pack up our car, giving up opening Santa's presents and leaving Grandma's at 5 a.m. on Christmas day. They wanted to go home to Dad and the snow. It was a lonely ten-hour drive home on Christmas day. I remember at lunchtime, we ate at the only restaurant open in Paris, Texas, which was a Denny's. Lunch at Denny's was not exactly what I had in mind for Christmas dinner. We were only three hours away from home and Thomas and Drew's excitement began to intensify. We started seeing cars coming down the highway covered in snow. Even the kid in *me* was coming out.

When we had finally arrived home, Dad was there to give Thomas and Drew a great big hug. Christmas presents were opened immediately. Though, our living room did not contain an atmosphere of joy. Jeff's mood was extremely somber and withdrawn. As evening drew near, we loaded up our car with sleds, chairs, and hot chocolate, taking the boys down to one of the local libraries to go sledding. We loved night sledding and the library had this incredible hill next to their parking lot, perfect for sledding. We must have stayed at least two hours. The hillside was packed with other people sledding who had the same idea as us. People were camped out with lawn chairs, hot drinks, and music! It was Christmas night. Though, Jeff and I hardly exchanged any words between us. There was a wall. There was distance between us. When we got home, our boys asked if they could sleep with us in our king size bed. They desperately missed their Dad and wanted to spend all of their time with him. He was their hero.

The next morning, Jeff woke up and quietly left our bedroom. He said he needed to get to outpatient therapy. I questioned him on what was going on between us. He said we would have a talk when he got home. I knew something was up. The boys spent the morning playing with their new stash of toys. There was junk scattered all over our house and it was just fine with me. My boys were home and they were happy. One of the greatest joys in my life is seeing my boys smile. It warms my heart more than anyone can ever imagine.

It was sometime after lunch when Jeff arrived home from therapy. He told the boys he needed to talk with mom and asked them to go upstairs and play in the game room for a while. Our lives were about to change once again. This time was forever. Jeff sat me down on our bed and began to tell me our marriage was over. He said he had been taking painkillers for the last eight years to escape the pain of being married to me. My jaw dropped, my heart sank and my ability to breath suddenly became difficult. I said you've got to give me a better excuse than that lame story. He then went on to share that God had given him the peace to leave his family. I told him, you better choose your words wisely to make that kind of statement in front of God. God does not nor will He ever give man peace to leave his family. It is stated many times in the Bible that God hates divorce. His mind was already made up and he packed his bags, hugged the boys goodbye and left. Just like that. Words cannot express how I felt at this time. Numbness was pretty good for starters. Initially, I thought this was just something he was going through and would snap out of it in due time.

I was beginning to wonder what in the world happened in detox to cause a man to change personalities. David Hudson had stopped by to visit Jeff on his last day of admission and noted he could visibly see a difference in him. It was almost as though he had been brainwashed. As the weeks and months passed, more people shared horror stories about this particular institution. How families' lives were changed or shattered. How they intermingled men and women together with different issues.

Later that evening, after Jeff walked out, three of his accountability partners from his Bible study group got in his face at Starbucks for about two hours. They told him over and over what a horrible mistake he was about to make and that he would regret it for the rest of his life. He refused to listen; his mind was made up. However, he did agree to counseling in exchange for a room at a hotel owned by one of his accountability partners, Daniel.

Daniel checked on Jeff daily. He had at least one meal with him every day and tried his hardest to keep Jeff accountable. Daniel was a dear friend who Jeff could not appreciate. Jeff was determined to end our marriage.

It was now New Year's week and our situation was not improving, to say the least. Daniel's wife, Kristie, had invited the boys and me to her parent's lake home on Grand Lake. I didn't feel like doing a single thing. I wanted to crawl in a hole but I had two boys who desperately needed their mother strong. I agreed to go up there for a few days to hibernate, get away and relax. Their property was rather large which allowed us the opportunity to spread out. Kristie had been such a source of encouragement for me. We developed a close friendship because of our situation with Jeff's opioid addiction. Another dear friend, Lauren, who was in my small group was so heartbroken that our family was not together for New Year's. In future chapters, you will read how Lauren became my treasure from God over the next few years. Please note, you are beginning to see more of God's Fingerprints dotted everywhere.

Lauren had spent New Year's Eve mourning our loss and feeling my pain. She said that God clearly spoke to her about me that evening. He said there would not be tears next New Year's Eve, but rather, rejoicing. I would be happy. You cannot imagine how I held onto those words for the entire year of 2003. It gave me hope. In fact, I changed the ring tone on my cell phone to "Auld Lang Syne." Every time my phone rang that tune, I was reminded of God's word for me.

The boys and I had about as nice a time as possible with our friends at Grand Lake. It even snowed on us New Year's Eve, which was a nice treat for my boys. We did come back to Tulsa the day after New Year's to find that Jeff had moved back home from the hotel. Though, things were not as I expected. He was extremely distant and hateful to me. He appeared to be there for the boys but was already emotionally checked-out with Thomas and Drew.

Here's another *I remember when…* I had just finished taking a relaxing, warm bath and came into our bedroom to find Jeff lying down on our bed watching TV. He began to tell me that he had met somebody in the hospital and thought he was already falling in love with her. He had already committed adultery and in his opinion, there was no room for turning back to his family. I'm not sure exactly how to put my feelings into words here. Betrayal once again was good for starters. It hurt because he had violated God and our wedding vows. However, it wasn't necessarily the kind of pain of *oh my gosh, the love of my life has left me*. By this point, after years of deception, the love I had for my husband had pretty much evaporated. Was this God protecting me because He knew this was going to happen? I don't know?

Needless to say, I didn't sleep at all that Friday night. Jeff went upstairs to sleep with Thomas. It would be his last night in our home. Shortly afterwards, Kristie came over to be with me. We spent several hours talking. Kristie did a lot of listening. If you don't know what to do or say when a friend is going through difficult circumstances, know that your listening ear and presence is a priceless gift. Kristie was a real friend to me. Later during the night, I went upstairs and got Jeff's cell phone. I found the telephone number of his new girlfriend and called her up. Looking back, I can't believe I was able to make that call but God gave me a certain drive to fight for my family. I asked her to please back off and allow God to work a miracle in our marriage for the sake of our sons. She didn't care to listen to anything I had to say, so I ended the conversation, telling her what I thought about her behavior before I hung up.

The next morning, Jeff became livid when he learned I called his girlfriend. He said I had done major damage. Whatever! Both Thomas and I were sick that day, running fever. I barely had the energy to take care of the boys, much less myself. Jeff must have spent the entire day on his cell phone in our backyard talking to her. I could not believe he had the nerve to rub his affair in his family's face. Jeff's girlfriend had gone to Kansas for the weekend and was so distraught over my phone call. He had to be with her. So he packed his bags and left his sick family to rush to her side. I asked him to at least stay and take care of Thomas who had thrown up most of the day. He didn't believe I was sick, so he threw the thermometer next to me and demanded I take my temperature. Well, lo and behold, Candy had a fever of 101 degrees. He then looked at the thermometer and basically said too bad, I've got to leave. At this point, his children didn't matter. Selfishly, all he could think of was his new girlfriend.

I was so glad and relieved the next day was Sunday. I could fall apart in my small group and feel safe with them. Most of our hour together was spent in prayer. As I was leaving church, Jeff called from his cell to let me know he was on his way home. My small group leader, William, immediately grabbed my phone to confront Jeff. After a little conversation, Jeff had agreed to meet with William in our home, along with whomever else, later that afternoon. Jeff's theory was that he was going to have to face everyone sooner or later; it might as well be now.

It was Sunday, January 5, 2003—my 9/11. It would be the longest day of my life. To this day, I have never experienced such a day of intense grief. William, his wife, Kathy, and Gerald from my small group all came over to confront Jeff. They were following God's instructions in 1st Timothy for two or more to confront a brother who has fallen into sin—thus allowing him the opportunity to repent. Another couple from our small group, Juan and Letty, came over to pick up Thomas and Drew, to bring them to the zoo. They needed to be out of the house for their emotional protection. The meeting between Jeff, William, and Gerald became ugly almost immediately. Kathy and I were in my bedroom praying. We heard shouting from behind closed doors. Gerald and William tried to reason with Jeff. He had already given his soul to the enemy and there was absolutely no reaching him. Jeff wanted to have his cake and eat it too, for a while, by living at home and carrying on with his affair. Gerald, a true gentle spirit, told Jeff it was time to hit the road. I did not have the emotional energy to do a thing. I was frozen. I was numb. William, Kathy, and Gerald warned Jeff of the dangers of leaving God, and that God's hand of protection would be removed from his life. He didn't care. So, I watched my dear friends kick my husband out of our home. My friends had shed so many tears and could not believe Jeff was choosing another woman over his own precious family. It felt like somebody had just died. I had that knot in my stomach that I only get when I'm at the funeral home after the death of a loved one. This time, it was the death of a family. My family.

Looking back at these moments, I am overwhelmed that God blessed me with dear friends who were able to stand in the gap with the boys and me. It was dirty work. They got messy. They were not "surface" friends who bolted when things got uncomfortable. I had one former friend, who was very close to our family, share that she just couldn't get involved and that she knew God would send others to help me in her absence. I would challenge you to look around at your circle of friends you currently have in your life. Nothing happens in life by coincidence. Friends that are planted in your life are there for a reason. When storms arise, you never know how God might use you to accomplish His purpose. Just think of the blessings we might miss out on if we bolted when seas get rough.

Looking back at these moments, I am overwhelmed that God blessed me with dear friends who were able to stand in the gap with the boys and me. It was dirty work. They got messy. They were not "surface" friends who bolted when things got uncomfortable.

I can remember that our associate pastor, Brother Henry, came over immediately to visit me after Jeff had been kicked out of our home. He said that during all of our many months of counseling together, he knew Jeff was not the least bit repentant. He would be happy to show me his notes after each of our sessions. Although, Henry was able to make me laugh. He commented, just think Sweetie, he didn't leave you for a beauty queen, but rather, he left you for someone he met in detox.

Perhaps there was a little comfort in Henry's statement. But I will never forget the next thing he asked me. He cupped his hands around my face and asked me what I wanted most. With tears flowing down my face, I said I wanted to be able to be home with my boys until they started the next school year in August. At that time, Drew would then be in first grade. That was eight months away. I passionately loved my job of being home with my boys, and when it came to their thoughts and feelings, my heart broke the most. Jeff had abandoned his boys. Their hearts were about to be shattered. How would it affect their lives? How would it shape their future? I couldn't bear the pain; I couldn't protect them from what was about to happen in their lives.

Oh how my heart ached deep down to the core of my soul. So, Henry said, that's the way we will pray, Candy. Jeff had been without a job since November. There was no sight of child support for the next few months. He admitted in detox that he had spent all of our savings on drugs in eight years. Our hard earned savings was gone! How in the world were we to survive financially, emotionally, and physically for the next eight months? Hang on; my story gets all the more interesting. Over the next year, God performed some major miracles. The kind of miracles that you read about in the Bible. Yes, He is still in the business of performing miracles in this modern age and I'm living proof.

I was not left alone for the next two days. There was such an incredible outpouring of love from my friends that you would not believe. They packed Jeff's clothes for me. They drove me to my bank to open up a new account. They escorted me to my attorney's office. They called my alarm company and made changes to our system. They called the locksmith—and on and on. They held me up when I couldn't do it alone. Yes, God's Fingerprints were being stamped all over the page; He was beginning to do a mighty work in my family. He was becoming my husband and a father to my boys as His word faithfully promises. My boys and I didn't ask to be abandoned.

I can now look back at these moments and know that Jeff's leaving was a blessing in disguise. Of course, God doesn't like divorce. However, God was aware of all of the many lies and acts of deception Jeff committed against our family over the years. I knew a lot about what Jeff did, but God knew everything. I tried everything humanly possible to help Jeff with his opioid addiction and made all attempts to save our marriage. I honestly think God had had enough. God knew that my heart was committed to my family. God knew I wouldn't walk away from the promises I made Him in my wedding vows to Jeff. With God's abounding grace and mercy, He carefully picked us up and removed us from Jeff's destructive path. The oppression began to slowly lift off of me during the next year. Over the next year, my physical appearance literally changed—like night and day. God was giving me the grace to be His bride.

CHAPTER 8

A Fairy Tale Neighborhood

"Because you have so little faith. Truly I tell you, if you have the faith as small as a mustard seed, you can say to this mountain, Move from here to there, and it will move. Nothing will be impossible for you."

— Matthew 17:20

I believe it's time to devote this small chapter to describe the most wonderful neighborhood in the world. It's very unusual. It's the type of neighborhood you heard about growing up in the '50s and '60s—a time when everyone looked after each other. You could go to sleep with your doors unlocked. You could borrow a cup of sugar without any problem. That's my neighborhood, Lexington Place; God dropped me here and not by accident. He knew the details of my future when we first moved here and how the events would unfold. He knew my boys and I would need lots of love and support.

Let me back up a bit, to describe how God's hand was in our move to Tulsa in 1998. Jeff accepted a regional management position with an construction firm in Tulsa, and as part of the compensation package, the company offered to fly us up there for a house-hunting trip. With deadlines at Jeff's job in Tyler, time would not allow him to make the trip. Instead, I took advantage of the opportunity and flew to Tulsa with a mission to find our home. We had just put our own house in Tyler on the market and we were attempting to sell by-owner. Some real estate agents just scoffed at that idea. Well, hello, God was involved!

I flew to Tulsa alone on a Friday night and was met at the airport by the HR manager and his family. They drove me to the office to pick up a company car and pointed me in the direction of my hotel. I was ready to grab the bull by the horns! I had already scheduled an appointment with a local real estate agent to pick me up at the hotel early Saturday morning to spend the day house hunting. Little did I know that God was going to bless me with the most wonderful agent who genuinely had my best interest in mind.

I woke up very early the next morning because I wanted to spend time with the Lord. I desperately needed His guidance, as I was about to embark on some major decisions that could affect my family's life, looking for not only a house but also a home. I asked God to guide me to His perfect home. I also asked God to bring the perfect buyer for our house in Tyler. So much needed to happen in a short period of time. It seemed almost overwhelming and impossible but not to God. He gave me such an incredible peace and comfort that everything in this move would fall into place according to His plan.

Two hours later, as I was about to walk out of my hotel to meet my agent, Jeff called to tell me that this sweet Christian lady had come by our house earlier that morning to make an offer. He wanted to take the offer immediately. Well, being the claims adjuster that I was, I wanted to negotiate. It was in my blood! We needed to get the best price we could because we were about to face some major expenses with a move. So, I called our potential buyer to discuss the details. She was a wonderful person and a believer. During our conversation, I found out that at the exact time I was praying earlier that morning for a buyer, God prompted her to drive by our house to see if the sign was still up in our yard. Wow, is that a God thing or what? And she also gave me an update on Thomas and Drew. She said they were happy, clean, their clothes appeared to match and Jeff was taking good care of them in my absence! Funny how there's always an unspoken bound between mothers.

God also allowed me to negotiate with her in bringing up her offer and paying all closing expenses. Jeff was floored at my negotiating abilities. I reminded him that it was not me but rather God, because His hand was definitely in this move. More Fingerprints from God! If we as believers take a leap of faith and trust God in following His will, there is absolutely nothing that will stop God in blessing you abundantly! He so delights when his children desire to follow and trust Him. He will knock your socks off!

My real estate agent and I spent the entire Saturday together and must have looked at a dozen houses. Yes, I was taking a leap of faith—I had only been to Tulsa once in my life and had no idea what this city had to offer our family. We drove through Tulsa when I was eleven years old, to attend my cousin's wedding in Bartlesville. Not much of an experience to base house-hunting on. During this time, I was videotaping the houses I liked, so that Jeff and I could view the houses together and make a decision when I flew home to Tyler the next week. I found our home. It was the last home we looked at on Saturday.

Here's another God-moment I must insert here. This home was in a nice neighborhood and the layout of the home was perfect. I mean *perfect*. It was on a dead-end corner, perfect for small children. There were sidewalks all over the neighborhood, perfect for small children. And, the elementary school was only one block away—also perfect for small children. Plus, I haven't even mentioned the neighborhood's most valuable asset, the people! This house had been on the market for six months. The interior was an ugly Barney-purple throughout the house, both upstairs and downstairs. Walls and carpet were purple! This house would not move even after the owning corporation lowered the price by $20,000.

Finally, the week before my house-hunting trip, the corporation agreed to paint and re-carpet the house a pleasant shade of taupe from top to bottom; thus making it a new home. All of the work was completed the day before I flew in. Word had gotten out in the real estate world that the "purple house" in Lexington Place was now a new house. That weekend, twelve buyers looked at the house and two bids were in on Monday morning! My agent called me early Monday morning with the news. She said if I wanted this house, I had to act fast. I thought to myself that I could not buy a house on my own without Jeff looking at it. Buying a house is usually the biggest purchase anyone will make in a lifetime. Help, God! Well, He did help me. He guided my steps and we were able to purchase our home. Little did I know, God was placing the boys and me on this particular block for a reason. He could see the future.

It's a little funny but true—our old friends, the Hudson family, who were instrumental in moving us from Tyler, Texas, said, God kept our house an ugly purple for six months until it was time for us to move. This house never moved for six months. God kept the corporation from making renovations until the perfect time. I truly believe God had His hand in each step of the way including the timing renovations were made to our house. Within three weeks of Jeff accepting the position in Tulsa, we had sold our house on our own in Tyler and purchased a new one in Tulsa. In fact, we had closed on both houses on the same day within two hours. The movers arrived at our new home the next day to unload our furniture and all of our worldly possessions. All of these events took place in two weeks and six days. Was God involved in moving mountains on behalf of our family? You bet! Like I mentioned earlier, if only you take a leap of faith and trust God, He will knock your socks off. I dare you, try it and see what happens!

God kept our house an ugly purple for six months until it was time for us to move.

Thirty-five kids lived on our new little street. There just happened to be an abundance of boys on our block; Thomas had seven friends on our street alone who were his age, and Drew had six. I'm not even mentioning kids on the other streets in our neighborhood.

When we moved in, we were welcomed with open arms. Cookies, cakes, pies, and sweets came flowing in through the front door—from strangers who were to become our best friends. Thomas immediately became best friends with our next-door neighbor, Kara. They were inseparable for the next eight months until Kara moved to Houston. Then, Nate, Sean, Wes, Elliot, and Marcus became his best friends. Even though Drew was only one year old at the time, he became friends with Nate's little sister, Allie. They became boyfriend and girlfriend through the years and were often nicknamed Adam and Eve. Their bedroom windows faced each other. Needless to say, we were able to fit into our new surroundings perfectly. Nearly all of the moms were stay-home moms; hence, we got to know each other very well. There were weekly playgroups, monthly bunko games and so on. We have truly lived life together, taking care of each other's families. Most of us are transplants from other states, therefore, we depended upon each other like family.

I have never had to worry about picking up my kids from school because of appointments or whatever else—we were there for each other, often picking up each other's kids. Whenever I was sick or had one of my many surgeries, my neighbors were always there with meals or to babysit; to run errands for me or take care of my lawn. You name it, it was done.

In the summers, we were always hanging out together, cooking out together, swimming together, and spending holidays together. We even knew each other's garage codes and helped ourselves if we needed something. We always operated on a pay-it-forward mode. Our kids could get away with absolutely nothing. Older ones of driving age, especially! We would "rat" on each other's kids in a good way. We were each other's eyes and ears. Meaning, our priority was our children's safety. We were all on the same page when it came to ethics and morals. There are at least two-dozen houses in our neighborhood my boys could run to if they needed to feel safe or were in trouble. The few friends who have moved away to different parts of the country have come back and said, there's no place like Lexington Place. Neighborhoods like ours just don't exist today.

We genuinely have deep compassion for each other. It's a God thing! God knew what He was doing when he carefully placed us in this neighborhood. My neighbors have been not only my best friends but also my rock and comfort through our storms.

CHAPTER 9

Now What

"Carry each other's burdens, and in this way you will fulfill the law of Christ."

— Galatians 6:2

Getting back to the story, it was January 2003 and I was separated from my husband. A term that I had a difficult time hearing out loud. Stuff like this happens to other people, not me. 2003 would be the most difficult year of my life yet—a year of many unknowns but in the same breath, a year of so many miracles. I wanted to give up so often. I sometimes had to pinch myself because I could not believe how my life had unfolded over the last few years. At least for now, the drama was over. The unknown oppression was gone. I no longer had to live in fear wondering if the bottom was going to fall out. I didn't have to hold my breath thinking what dark secret I would learn next from Jeff. Enough, I was tired. I was weary. I wanted the pain to go away for good. I wanted God to make it all better. Whenever I looked into Thomas and Drew's tender eyes, I was always able to find strength to get up. I didn't have a choice. No more deception. Finally, I could live life without fearing the next act of deception from Jeff. I was determined that the enemy would not defeat our family. I had God on my side. It was His battle and that battle had already been won on the cross. I was desperately grabbing ahold of God's promises.

Shortly after Jeff left our family, our friend, David Hudson, made an observation. He said, Candy, in your last trial God brought you to your knees during your sickness. He made you strong. Your walk grew by leaps and bounds. Praise God for your ten-month illness because it has given you the strength to handle this new trial of epic proportions. I thought to myself he was absolutely correct. There was no way on God's green earth that I could have been prepared for Jeff's departure emotionally or spiritually without my last trial. But at the same time, I wanted to say God stop it, enough trials! I beg of you, I don't want any more trials relatively close to this magnitude. Yes, I'm aware that we will face various trials until we get to the other side but I'm hoping I will never face this road again.

Praise God for your ten-month illness because it has given you the strength to handle this new trial of epic proportions.

It was now my first week to live life as a single parent. How in the world would I survive? How were my boys going to survive? The first thing William and Kathy gave to me was the greatest gift anyone could have given me. They had given me ten counseling sessions with their Christian counselor who is so anointed in doing God's work. Initially, I thought to myself that I didn't need counseling. I wasn't the one with problems. Besides, I had never spent any time on the "couch". I think years ago Americans use to view therapy or counseling as a weakness. Oh quite the contrary, it's a sign of strength to admit that you need help. When one has a cold, one visits their family doctor. If you break your arm, you'll more than likely visit an orthopedic surgeon. If your tooth hurts, you will make a trip to your dentist. So, why is it when our hearts are broken, we don't get them fixed with counseling? Is it a pride thing or perhaps an issue of ignorance? Regardless, I wish more people had the wisdom to seek out counseling. I will say that William and Kathy's gift was the best investment made in me. Another Fingerprint! It was the beginning of getting emotionally healed. I needed to learn the skills on how to survive, and not simply to cope. Jesus never did cope. He dealt with the issues head on. Too many people try to get over traumatic events in their life by burying the pain. Not dealing with it. Not talking about it. If you do something in order to not feel any pain, then you are coping. Coping is not healing. That is the worst thing a person can do because it will eventually come out in the forms of a midlife crisis, divorce, abuse, addiction, panic attacks or whatever. But bottom line, it will come out and it will be uglier the longer it remains buried. I cannot stress here enough how valuable counseling is following a traumatic event. Kids need it even more if there were painful events during childhood.

Life during these first few months after he left was very difficult. It was an ongoing agony that wouldn't go away. I was in survival mode. There was a certain fog in the air and I was unable to see clearly. My dear friends began to take charge, hold my hand, and guide my steps. It seemed as though I was fighting battles daily. What next? Every time I would turn around, there was another flame to put out. These days became the norm for the next few years. You learn to adjust, even against your own will. Unfortunately (and fortunately, too), only a person who has been through a divorce can understand the depth of this pain. It doesn't make sense. As the next few days, weeks, and months began to unfold before my eyes, I could truly understand why God hates divorce. It affects everything about your existence, your personhood, your self worth and so on.

The most painful consequence is to helplessly watch your children suffer. You cannot do a darn thing to make it better. Sure, you can be there to love and support them, but the fabric of their very existence has been destroyed. All I could think of during these days was what was going to happen to Thomas and Drew's future as adults. Would there be any permanent damage? Would they have difficulty in relationships as adults? How were they going to treat women? When will it come out? Would they repeat the same pattern as their father? I was determined that this generational curse would end with Jeff. My boys belonged to Christ. In later chapters, I'll share about a word God gave me during a dream. It was a reference to Daniel 3 in the Bible about three young men who survived a furnace—God Himself delivered them from a horrible trial. I was given that same promise for the boys and me. Would I trust God through the difficult moments over the next few years? Would I remember His promise?

Kathy spent that very first night with me, January 5, 2003. I was thankful I didn't have to spend my first few nights alone. Do you see the Fingerprints? Along with Penny and Gerald from our small group, we prayed for peace and safety over our home. Jeff had allowed the enemy a strong foothold into our home for such a long period. It was time to clean house! We also spent time in both Thomas and Drew's rooms praying over them and dedicating them to the Lord. As parents, we have supernatural authority over our children. They have a blanket of protection under us. It is our duty and responsibility as parents to protect our children. Our own actions and behavior affect our children whether we like it or not. I walked into their bedrooms every night after they had fallen asleep dedicating them to Christ and praying over them. There is so much power in a mother's prayer over her children, and I am committed to praying for my boys for the rest of my life. I started praying for Godly wives the moment they were born. I also pray that God will cross their paths with Godly counsel and mentors all of their days. We can never pray too much over our children! God does hear our prayers.

It was time for my counseling to begin. It had been four long days since Jeff had left our family. I had my first appointment with Janet. I will stop right here and say Janet was instrumental in saving my life. She gave me the tools to survive, from a Biblical point of view. So many of her examples and references were of Christ. He truly suffered every kind of trial we as human beings experience here on earth. I'll admit, it did take a few weeks of counseling to see some Ah-Ha moments. It is remarkable and amazing to see how a trained counselor can take areas of your life that you've never understood for years and make perfect sense of them. She helped me to see that I was really God's treasure and I mattered to Him. She said she was going to fix me if I allowed her to so that I wouldn't be attracted to the same type of guy next time around. Oh, let's hope so! I was determined to never ever allow another man to treat me with such disrespect. If I ever find the courage to marry again, my desire is to find someone, in God's perfect timing, who is stronger in the Lord than me and who will treat me with the utmost dignity and respect. Learning how to trust someone with the honesty issue will be my hardest challenge, personally. I'm quite sensitive (and with good reason!) to the honesty thing.

Janet also dug deep into the pits of my own family, where I discovered troubled areas that I was not aware of or that didn't make much sense to me. Bottom line: Every family has areas of weakness. We are a work in process; under construction. If you can identify these areas, then you can only gain from this insight.

I saw Janet on a weekly basis over the next four months. I actually looked forward to my counseling sessions with her. I could relax and be myself. It was a safe place to share my fears. She stretched me as a person. Then, I started group therapy for the next ten weeks. I will discuss this group study in a later chapter. All I can say is oh my, it was one of the most beneficial studies I ever took part in during my life. It helped me to become not only a better person but also a better parent. My outlook on counseling and therapy changed completely. So much emotional healing took place. Again, I cannot recommend counseling enough, particularly from a Christian's perspective.

It was February 2003, and I was getting ready for yet another surgery. This was the first time I didn't have a husband to hold my hand. Yes, I had my mother to fly up and was surrounded by many friends but it wasn't the same. I didn't have a partner by my side. Though, I will say that due to the circumstances, I didn't want Jeff by my side either. It was the companionship and the support of a spouse that I greatly missed. This time around, my surgery was on an outpatient basis; therefore, recovery was quicker. My neighbors were wonderful as usual with meals, babysitting, and mochas. I will admit that mochas are my weakness. It's my treat! All of my dearest and nearest friends know this particular fact about me. I cannot begin to count the number of mochas that have been delivered on my doorstep over the years and especially during this trial. It might sound insignificant to some, but God truly cares about the little details in our lives. I call them little "Valentines" from God!

My neighbors made arrangements to have my boys sleep over that first night I was home from the hospital; thus, giving me time to recuperate. However, there were many harassing calls that afternoon and evening from Jeff. Nothing makes sense with an addict in the picture. They are unable to rationalize and can cause lots of unnecessary grief. This would become the norm for Jeff over the next few years. He never knew when to stop with the verbal abuse. At this point, I never gave him the time of day, stopping any type of communication, which I believe angered him. It appeared he thrived on confrontation, whereas I didn't.

I call them little "Valentines" from God!

A week after my surgery was Valentine's Day. I had mediation scheduled at my attorney's office. This was not how I wanted to spend my Valentine's. I had always been available for Thomas and Drew's parties at school. This was the first time I missed their parties, and I felt robbed of not being able to attend. Before leaving my house for mediation, I can remember sitting alone in my dining room. I sat there for a few moments to be still. I looked around thinking this is not how I imagined my life.

God clearly spoke to me in an audible voice and said, I promise next year will be better.

Mediation wore me out physically, emotionally, and mentally, as it lasted approximately four hours. Plus, I was still recovering from surgery. I couldn't even bring myself to look at Jeff from across the table. He looked so evil. Decisions were made during mediation, though, Jeff never once adhered to those decisions. It didn't come as a surprise to me but with cruel and inconvenient timing (Valentine's Day), he filed for divorce during mediation. *While he added salt to my wounds, it would become a blessing in disguise.*

CHAPTER 10

An Important Neighbor

"For I know the plans I have for you, declares the Lord, plans to prosper you and not harm you, plans to give you hope and a future."

— JEREMIAH 29:11

I SURVIVED MEDIATION. I was being sued for divorce from my husband of sixteen years. Spring was only a month away. Life continued to unravel and take unnatural courses. This part of my life was never on my radar screen. It didn't make any sense; I didn't understand why God kept allowing things to get worse as I kept drawing closer to Him. What was His plan for me? I was learning a difficult lesson of who was truly in control. Definitely not me! I was being pruned and shaped: I know God does some of his best work while we're in the valleys but it's not pleasant. In the book of James, Paul states that we as believers should rejoice in our sufferings and trials. Although I was definitely not "there," or anywhere close to rejoicing, my attitude did begin to shift over time. It's a process. It's a journey. I was being refined and polished into becoming more Christ-like. Often, shattered dreams are the only avenue toward spiritual growth. Sometimes it might be difficult to discover our true desire for God if things are going well, right?

Shortly after mediation, I had a conversation (not by accident) with my next-door neighbor, Linda, about another neighbor on our street, Ann. I know God moved it upon Linda's heart to share with me some concerns regarding Ann—whom I knew as my neighbor but not very well because we didn't have children the same ages. She had been a stay-home mom raising girls who were a few years older than my boys. Ann was beginning to experience some of the same grief that I had experienced—namely, an unhappy marriage with an unfaithful husband. Unfortunately, Ann and I now had undesirable things in common. Linda thought we might be able to relate with each other's difficult life circumstances.

Often, shattered dreams are the only avenue toward spiritual growth.

After talking with Linda, I strongly felt the urge to reach out to Ann because I could only imagine what she was experiencing. Within an hour, I was sitting in Ann's living room and we were sharing our stories. Little did either one of us know that this would be the beginning of a God-created friendship and business partnership. Oh, just to look back now and see how God orchestrated and weaved our friendship is supernatural. I now know that God's hand was in our friendship. We complement each other in so many ways. As you continue reading more about Ann, you will find multiple Fingerprints!

The very next week, Ann called me to have an early dinner with a mutual friend from our block, Missy, who had gone through a similar situation a few years earlier, with a cheating and abusive husband. Missy had made it to the "other-side"—aka life after divorce. Missy had been a stay-home mom for over fifteen years raising three kids. A similar story repeated more often than imagined. She was left with basically nothing and had to start over. At that time, Ann's husband hired Missy in his company. As she learned the durable medical equipment business, she soon branched out with her own business fitting patients with orthopedic braces. Missy is an inspiration to all; her compassion to help others is remarkable. God has blessed her in so many ways, and she now has a real desire to help others going through situations like her own.

At dinner that evening, Missy offered me the opportunity to work part-time for her, thus giving me the flexibility to still be available for my boys if they needed me. It had been years since I had worked outside of the home. These were baby steps for me. I wasn't afraid of working. I was afraid of not being available for my boys. They are my world and greatest treasure.

Two weeks later, I found myself working part-time. God's timing was perfect. I needed this boost, to rebuild my self-esteem and re-claim some dignity that was lost. I was all too reminded of a verse in 1Peter 5:10—*The God of all grace will Himself restore you and make you strong, firm and steadfast.* Glimpses of His perfect promises were being delivered; I just needed to stand still and feel my Father's presence. That was a challenge for me. I am guilty of "busyness" in my life, trial or no trial. If only we would slow down and be still, we would hear from God more often. Sounds simple but why do we struggle being still? He has never left our side nor will He ever leave us.

Drew was in half day Kindergarten in the afternoons during this time. Missy was so gracious to allow Drew to come to work with me in the mornings; it was a treat for both of us. I mean really, how many employers would allow you to bring your child to work with you? Another sweet Fingerprint from God!

I was desperately seeking God's guidance, and He was beginning to open my eyes up to my future. I knew deep within my heart the baby steps had to end. I needed more stability for my family. Paying child support didn't appear to be an option or a desire for Jeff. Part of me wanted to become very bitter towards him but I couldn't allow anger to fester within me, as it wouldn't be healthy for my boys. It was not about me. I had to give these raw emotions over to God and allow Him to deal with Jeff accordingly. God told me over and over He would take care of us. It was up to me. Would I step out on faith and completely trust Him? Much easier said, right? Janet, my counselor, would always ask me the same question at the end of each of our sessions, Hasn't God provided for you so far? Of course, the answer was always yes. Then, she would follow up with the same next question, Why would He stop now? She was always right and said what made the most sense to me—a kind of sense that gave me the hope to hang onto Christ. I had nowhere else to turn. And what is so amazingly cool is that God really does reward His children for their total obedience. Of course we are going to have slip ups along the way. Though, have we determined in our heart to be completely obedient? God is the only one who knows your heart and your inner most thoughts.

Little did I know God was guiding me down the road to entrepreneurship. My neighbor, Ann, and I were beginning to explore our options in starting a medical billing business. I didn't have the funds; she did. Though, I had the knowledge of dealing with medical claims. I was beginning to see some Ah-ha's for the first time, regarding some of the paths I had taken over the last eighteen years in my life. Every single job I have had, whether part-time or full-time, had been medical related. My last position was as an injury claims adjuster with State Farm for seven years. I gained a wealth of experience and knowledge from that job. God knew exactly how my life was going to unfold in future years and He began preparing me to own a medical billing business without me even suspecting a thing. Wow! I always knew God worked behind the scenes, but it was then that I could actually see the proof through my life. So often, we may think God is not doing anything, or we'll actually question if He really hears our prayers. God is always at work; though, often His work is unseen. That's where faith steps in for us. Are we going to trust Him? Step out in faith?

Ann and I decided to cast our lots together. We found ourselves in similar situations and knew we were two college educated stay-home Moms who had some talent to offer. So together, we pooled our resources and began the process of starting our own business. This is probably one of the biggest Fingerprints you will read in this book. I would not be in business if it were not for the kindness and compassion of a dear friend. When I think of a word to describe Ann, "giving" comes to mind. I could write a separate book on her sweet generosity.

CHAPTER 11

Group Therapy

"Now I will break their yoke from your neck and tear your shackles away."

— Nahum 1:13

I want to dedicate a chapter in this book to group therapy because it made such a positive impact in my life. God did not intend for our world to be so messed up. He did not intend for us to live with broken hearts. He did not intend for divorce. He did not intend for midlife crises to take place; hence, leaving a wake of destruction for innocent family members to pick up the pieces. I was able to witness first hand during group therapy what happens to adults when traumatic things happen in childhood. Often, a lot of delayed pain that resurfaces later in life.

I was in the middle of intense counseling with Janet when she started one of her group therapy classes called "Making Peace with your Past." For weeks, she would suggest the class to me; she thought it would be not only beneficial but also healthy. Group therapy is yet another layer in counseling which offers critical support. She said it would make me a better parent. Ok, she then hit a nerve. I was all for becoming a better parent to my boys. But in my opinion, there was one major problem. The class lasted for ten long weeks. Each session was approximately three hours. How in the world was I going to swing that with my boys and baseball season just beginning? Between two boys, I had at least thirty games on the schedule! I was not Super Mom; although, at times I felt like it. Once again, Janet would come back with her deep words of wisdom, If God wants you to be there, then everything will fall into place with your boys being taken care of while you're at group.

So, the following Sunday during my small group, I voiced my request regarding group therapy. Within a week, I had volunteers offering to watch Thomas and Drew for all ten sessions. At this point, I didn't have any real excuses keeping me from group therapy. God definitely wanted me to join this group. Can you see more Fingerprints?

Many live on anti-depressants and opioids to medicate the pain. If you do not fully let go of your past, how can you move forward and accomplish all that God has planned for your life? We can choose to be fully bound up in our past, live in pity parties and blame everything else or choose to rise up and use the resources available to us such as counseling and group therapy.

I remember driving to my first group session. I was a bit nervous and apprehensive. I knew I would have to talk about painful and uncomfortable things. Janet said everybody talks during group therapy. I knew she wasn't kidding! She doesn't let anyone escape. How else can you heal if you don't talk about it? When I walked into the room, I saw our name-tags spread out on both sofas and chairs throughout the room. Initially, I felt as though I was on a Bob Newhart show from the '70s and Carol would walk in and offer us refreshments or something. Of course, all of Bob's patients on TV were nuts. I wasn't and the people I saw in the room appeared normal. Almost immediately, the six of us had a bond. We clicked. Janet commented that our immediate closeness was rare in her group therapy sessions. Usually, it takes several weeks for everyone to feel comfortable in revealing the vulnerable sides from within. Another Fingerprint.

Each one of us had a unique and heartbreaking story. Though, we had a common bond: unsolicited pain. As the weeks passed, I began to notice another common denominator. There was some childhood event that triggered or contributed to the current situation. Some came from divorced homes; some neglected as children; another home had alcoholism; one lost a parent at a young age; one lost a spouse to suicide, and so on. In all honesty, I probably came from the healthiest home. I grew up in a very traditional Southern Baptist home. There were no problems related to addictions, abuse, or divorce. I felt lots of love. My family has a wonderful Christian heritage. Janet even commented that my type is the hardest case to crack. In other words, there were no major, outwards signs of problems that came from within my home. In fact, I have very fond memories of my childhood growing up on a rice farm. I was my father's princess and could do no wrong. Perhaps that was part of the problem. As a child, I managed to get away with a lot more than I should have. My parents were older, my only sibling was ten years older and most relatives were much older. However, it was not my fault that my birth order came many years later. Now being a parent, I can relate. You are much stricter with the first child, and as time goes on, the parent within you begins to lighten up, you mellow, and you wear down! By the time I came around, the sky was the limit. Please understand, I mean absolutely no disrespect towards my parents. They were wonderful and raised me to know the Lord. The greatest gift a parent can impart on their child is introducing them to Jesus and leading by example. Much of what I learned from my parents was "caught."

As the weeks progressed on in our "Making Peace with your Past" class, conversations grew much deeper. Everyone became incredibly transparent. During this trial, I think I have learned that one of the most important characteristics in any relationship is transparency. It doesn't matter if the relationship is between spouses, children, or friends. Once the wall is broken down, you can do life deeply with that person. After all, God created us to be dependent upon each other, like the body of Christ, rather than the world's view of independence. You can then allow God the opportunity to strengthen your relationship. Unfortunately, most of us do not bring down walls due to fear of rejection. There is always a reason for that underlying fear. It does not and never will happen by chance. What event or events in your life brought on the human feeling of fear? More than likely it was events during your childhood—the formative years. Children from divorced homes may have difficulty with relationships as adults. The family unit is the core of a child's existence. If that is broken, then what's to keep it from happening in their adult life? A level of fear is being formed at a young age. If the fear is never dealt with in the form of discussion, like in counseling, then more than likely it will be allowed to grow into perhaps a big, bad monster. This same idea of fear applies in death, an accident, alcoholism, or abuse.

In group therapy, I was able to witness how fear and rejection played a significant role in everyone's lives. In some people, it was hardly noticeable if at all. In others, it was obvious. Then, there are dozens of characteristics that are by-products of fear. These characteristics form and grow over the years, often unnoticed until it's too late. These characteristics can hinder us from moving forward into healthy relationships. We sometimes miss out on so many wonderful blessings and opportunities.

However, there is great news! No problem is ever too big for God or counseling. It may be a long process. It will probably be a painful process. At one time, these feelings were painful as you buried them in the "vault." A person usually copes with these types of emotions and feelings through the burial process of silence. Let's not talk about it. Denying your emotional past gets in the way of developing present intimacy. Self-protection is both wrong and foolish when looking at the big picture. If you're going to get healthy and face your fears, then you will have to excavate those feelings, which will be painful once again. But, the rewards are worth it. You will be set free from the bondage of fear and all of its by-products including rejection, loneliness, depression, anxiety, and so on. You will become a stronger person. You will be emotionally healthy, with the wonderful opportunity to sustain healthy relationships. Counseling is a sign of strength rather than weakness.

Due to the above paragraphs, Thomas and Drew have been seeing a counselor since their father walked out on them. I want them to deal with all of these issues head on now as children rather than resurfacing as adults. I do not want them to repeat or struggle with their father's stronghold of addiction. Many of their sessions have been painful. And, I will also say, there have been some sessions where I could hear their sweet laughter coming through the walls. I know deep down in my heart I am doing the right thing by keeping them in counseling. It may be a long time before we will see the rewards and benefits of counseling, but I am willing to wait. My hope is in God and I choose life. I can see great things in Thomas and Drew's future. I strongly feel the Lord will use them to help others in similar situations down the road, which reminds me of Romans 8:28.

Counseling is a sign of strength rather than weakness.

CHAPTER 12

2003, A Year to Forget

"A father to the fatherless, a defender of widows is God in his holy dwelling."

— Psalm 68:5

2003 WILL PROBABLY BE recorded in my mental history book as the worst year of my life. It began with my husband of sixteen years walking out on me. I was faced with an unfamiliar season in life—being a single, broke mother.

I had been a stay-home mom for years, depending on my husband to financially provide for our family. My year ended pretty much the way it began, horrible. It ended with an ugly trial resulting with a finalized divorce. However, I'm having a little difficulty saying I want to forget this year because God moved some major mountains on my behalf. I cannot deny God's mighty work and power. It is our responsibility to share with others what God does in our lives. It's all part of the Great Commission, mentioned in Matthew 28:19.

Initially, when our world started tumbling down, our immediate family in Louisiana strongly urged me to move home. I have always missed living near my family, but the thought of moving home just didn't seem like an option. It didn't feel right nor did it feel like home anymore. It had been over thirteen years since I lived in Louisiana. When your life is falling apart, loved ones want to step in with good intentions and attempt to fix things for you. My situation was not fixable at the moment. I was even told that there was no way I could take care of my boys by myself. Of course, that statement crushed me. I wanted to say, watch me! I knew

I couldn't do it alone, but with God's help, I had a chance. However, I didn't want to rule out moving back to Louisiana if that option was part of God's plan. I was willing to go anywhere he wanted me to move. I spent a lot of time in prayer seeking God's direction about my family's future. He told me I was exactly where I needed to be. I was already home in Tulsa. Looking back now, it was my only option. Our home and neighborhood was the stability my boys desperately needed at the time. They loved going to school. Everything was the same at school; nothing had changed. Nobody left or abandoned them at school. My neighbors were wonderful and extended their loving arms to Thomas and Drew. There wasn't a single day that didn't go by without an act of kindness from one of my neighbors—picking up groceries, watching my boys, carpooling, bringing them to sporting events or meetings, walking over a mocha, a phone call with a listening ear or an afternoon sitting around talking with friends. The kindness never ceased. That was God Himself, using friends to reach out to us; thus, God keeping His promise to take care of us.

My small group from church reached out in so many ways as well. They held my hand so many times when I was weak. The biggest lessons I have learned from this ugly trial is humility, waiting on God and remaining in a "place" where He wants me. I think this is what we call perseverance.

Too often, we want to do everything possible to not feel the pain by medicating it—with relationships, staying busy with your children, work, school or physical activities. Christians are just as guilty by staying involved in church activities for the wrong reasons. I know I wanted my pain to end. Janet reminded me that God had me in this place for a reason. Let Him do His work. If it were in my best interest to remove me from this place, He would have already taken me out of it. He was more interested in refining my character. Oh, I did not want to hear those words but deep down I knew there was truth in Janet's comments. If we deny our pain, then we truly remain unaware of our innermost desire for God. Suffering still provides a vital function in our walk. Suffering moves us away from demanding what is good toward the desire of what is better. Our appetite for God may become more apparent.

I had a difficult time accepting gifts from others. I guess you could describe my reluctance as pride. Janet always reminded me during counseling that humility is a characteristic of Christ. Christ came to earth to serve and not be served. He faced every type of trial we as humans face but on a much deeper level. I wanted to be independent but God wanted me to be dependent upon Him. This was such a hard concept for me to grasp since the "world" views independence as a strength and dependence as a weakness. The world wanted me to go out there and get a nine-to-five job but God had other plans for me. He was testing my faith. My boys needed their Mom desperately as this was not your normal divorce. Dad was their hero and in the blink of an eye, he was gone. Their adulthood was in jeopardy.

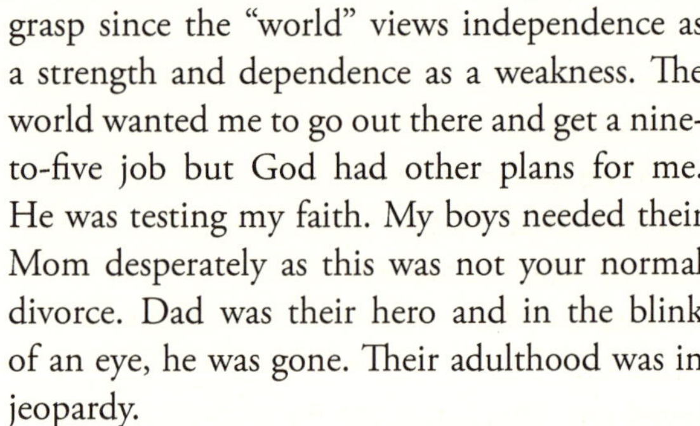

Suffering still provides a vital function in our walk. Suffering moves us away from demanding what is good toward the desire of what is better. Our appetite for God may become more apparent.

It was definitely a faith-walk for me. Times were difficult when loved ones with good intentions would lay on pressure for me to do what they thought was best for my family. There were suggestions here and there. Again, I mean no disrespect towards anyone because I know his or her intentions were in the right place. I had to listen to God and nobody else.

2003 consisted of miracle after miracle. It's rather hard to explain how a family of three survived on little-to-no income and was able to remain in our home.

Here's the faith walk. I know I will not be able to give you, the reader, a full picture of the many miracles that took place but I will try to touch on some of them. A precious friend paid my mortgage for an entire year. My jaw still drops when I think about that miracle. Was that God in a mighty and gracious way or what? Bills were paid anonymously on my behalf. Gift certificates to Walmart trickled in throughout the year. A dear, sweet family who I hadn't seen in years dropped a $1,000 check in the mail with a note saying we love you, hang in there and we're praying for you. Words cannot express how an expression of love like that makes you feel until it happens to you.

Another family out of state mailed me a $300 gift certificate from Toys "R" Us during the holidays to help my boys have a great Christmas. Another family from our church brought us along with their family to Silver Dollar City in Branson, Missouri several times to give our family little escapes from everyday life. My boys had given up so much. Friends helped me with my yard work. Friends helped me with my housework.

Maid-service was given to me several times. Gift cards from gasoline stations appeared in my mailbox or doorstep. Gifts in the form of toys or video games were given to my boys from time to time with anonymous notes saying you are loved. A great percentage of my legal fees were taken care of by dear friends.

One particular moment still brings tears to my eyes. It happened at our church on Mother's Day. One of my friend's dads found Thomas in his Sunday school classroom and slipped him some money. He told Thomas to treat his Mom to lunch. Wow! Again, words cannot describe how this made me feel. It was God wrapping His arms around me telling me He loved me. This is just the tip of the iceberg of the many Fingerprints our family received from God. This is exactly where God wanted me and He rewarded me so many times for my obedience to Him. He was building my character. Oh, was He ever! Janet also reminded me so often that God was using me as well to bless others. Giving is more of a blessing than receiving. She said my humility was allowing others to receive a blessing. To this day, every time I receive a gift from another believer, I am reminded of Galatians 6:10: *Therefore, as we have the opportunity, let us do good to all people, especially to those who belong to the family of believers.*

I have often said that the amount of friends who have stood in the gap for me is supernatural. I'm not talking about just a handful of friends. I mean nobody has dozens of close friends in their life. This is all supernatural and it's all about God and NOT about Candy! God is the hero in this story and I give Him all of the praise. I long for the day when I can pay forward and help others. Perhaps this book will be the beginning; thus encouraging others during dark hours.

God speaks to me not only through friends but also through nature. I often feel closest to my Father when I'm outdoors taking in my surroundings. Whether it's driving down a beautiful winding, country road on an autumn day or soaring over waves on a jet ski, I love God's paintbrush illustrated in nature. Nothing can duplicate it!

> ***God is the hero in this story and I give Him all of the praise.***

I remember driving home with my neighbor, Ann, one summer evening down the Muskogee turnpike. We were coming from Locust Grove. I had to see for myself what kind of place Jeff was living in to cause him to abandon his boys. Understanding that our marriage was over was not the problem. I had trouble understanding how a father could just walk away from his own flesh and blood, innocent children. It didn't make any sense to me. The campground environment he lived in was like night and day when contrasted with our neighborhood.

While driving home, I had an incredible knot in my stomach. Life was hard and I had a difficult time seeing the road ahead of me. But out of nowhere came this most incredible, beautiful sunset. It was so vast and full of many shades of pink, red, orange and blue. I cannot put into words how the light weaved in and out of the clouds. The sunshine became ribbons of color. You could see rays of light shooting in every direction. It was at that very moment I could hear God speaking to me in an audible voice, You are going to be just fine; I am taking care of you, my child! I felt His mighty presence as though I could feel His breath. Ann and I were in awe for at least thirty minutes as we drove into the sunset. And I mean *literally* because the sunset gradually disappeared in front of us. That sunset became symbolic as God's promise that He would take care of me. So, every single time I see a sunset, my breath is taken away. It's God's message to me. In fact, I took a picture of that sunset and have that very picture displayed on my desk today. I'm reminded of his promise every morning when I sit at my desk to work.

2003 seemed to be the year that would never end. Some years appear to breeze by in a blink of an eye, but time just seemed to linger at times, it stood still for me. Life moved at a snail's pace. Typically, I am the type of person who moves slowly toward every major decision in life. It must be researched, analyzed, scrutinized and so forth. Sometimes, I can drive others crazy, but that's just the way God created me. I like to take my time with life, but due to the ongoing agony in our lives, life appeared to be moving just too slow. I felt as though I needed to take over some areas of my life. Wrong, wrong, wrong! Bad move on my part. Though, we live and learn through our mistakes. right? This is where God's grace can shine through us.

CHAPTER 13

Wrong Detours Taken

"Walk with the wise and become wise, for a companion of fools suffers harm."

— Proverbs 13:20

There are some areas I hesitate to discuss in this book; though, I would like for others to learn from my mistakes. Sometimes, we have to make these mistakes on our own to learn from them. Adults are no different than children in this area. It's all part of the journey. I keep telling myself I've been so transparent in this book thus far, why stop now? It's about yielding versus rebelling. It's black and white. Do we give in to our fleshly desires and customize God's word to fit our needs? And there's a very good word for this: hypocrisy! Do we dare try to manipulate God? He won't stand for it and eventually, the flames from the fire will get too hot for us. Do we become so desensitized with lies and deception from the enemy that we can't see straight? By this time, can we even recognize when we are being deceived? And with all of this above-mentioned crud, do we block God's blessings upon our lives? I sure did!

It had been nearly a year of living alone without my husband, companion, and best friend. It's just something nobody can understand unless they walk in these shoes. I was beginning to feel lonely and missed companionship. I'm not necessarily describing sex here but I am talking about the types of intimacies you get from a relationship with your spouse. These are things like in-depth discussions, being heard, being complimented, being appreciated, working as a team, sharing stories together, sharing life together, having a back rub or just being pampered.

I thought I might be ready for dating but then again, yuck! It had been nearly twenty years since I dated, and I didn't have a clue what I was in store for me, stepping back into the world of dating. Surely I would be much wiser this time around; after all, I had the wisdom of eighteen years since I was last here. Oh my: wrong! The rules hadn't changed much nor the games. Even at my age. And, most important of all, where in the heck do you meet people, at a bar? I think not! At church? Many churches don't have active single groups for adults.

One night, while goofing around on my computer, I stumbled across an Internet dating site. I entered my zip code and wow! There were a lot of decent-looking guys posted on this site from my area. These guys even looked fairly normal! Initially, it seemed almost too good to be true. That should have been clue number one for me. If it seems too good to be true, it probably is. However, with the internet available 24/7 and the way our lives have become so busy, Internet dating has become very common in our society. It's easy; you can begin the dating process in the comfort of your own home, without putting on makeup and getting ready. Sometimes, it's too convenient; meaning, it can also be a lazy form of dating. Before you go out on that first date, you can get to know somebody fairly well through lots of emails and telephone conversations. It seems like a good deal to some. Though, many who are not in the dating world don't have a clue what it's like.

I will admit that a few of my first dates came from meeting local people on the Internet. It's kind of weird and neat at the same time. I would always meet in very crowded places like restaurants for dinner or dessert. Though, I made one fatal mistake. I started this process while I was separated, only two months before my divorce was finalized. I know to the world it was no big deal. Everyone is doing it, right? After all, my husband had left me. However, to God, it was a big deal. I was still married in His eyes even though Jeff had violated our vows. My yielding to God was beginning to vanish. I was having small glimpses of God withholding blessings from my life. He does reprimand His children for their disobedience only because He loves us so much! At times, I was reminded of Jeremiah 30:11, *I will discipline you but only with justice; I will not let you go entirely unpunished.*

However, I tended to ignore that part of scripture. I was customizing God's word to fit my wants and needs rather than depending upon Him.

In light of this, I am very thankful I had a dear accountability friend, Lauren, from my small group, who never judged me but told me what she thought about my dating before my divorce was finalized. She always backed up everything she told me with scripture. I loved her dearly for genuinely caring for me, but there were also times I didn't want to hear the truth from her. Though, I must share her catch phrase she often quoted that still makes me laugh to this day. Most of the guys I dated were drop-dead gorgeous. Lauren would come back and say they were just a hot fudge sundae with lots of window dressing delivered from Satan. Oh, I had to laugh and yet I couldn't stand it when she would say those things. I must admit, looking back, she had a colorful way of describing the truth! Of course, the enemy wouldn't send an ugly date my way—where's the temptation there!?

I was customizing God's word to fit my wants and needs rather than depending upon him.

A new chapter in my life began on December 3, 2003. This was the day of my trial. My attorney advised me that when my trial was over, I would walk out of the courtroom officially divorced. I was so looking forward to closure, but at the same time, I dreaded being put on the witness stand. I wasn't looking forward to dredging up the ugly past nor was I looking forward to seeing Jeff. My trial lasted six long hours which seemed to last an eternity. I was on the witness stand for over two hours and I shined. I could feel the power of the Holy Spirit all through me. I wasn't nervous and I remained incredibly calm through the entire questioning process from both sides. I was totally blown away by my calmness on the stand.

God spoke through me; some of what came out of my mouth was not me. At one point, my attorney had given me a huge binder with all of the evidence in it. He had asked me various questions from the binder. As he continued to question me on the stand, I began doodling all over one page with God "graffiti" writing things like God Rules, He is Faithful, He is a God of Justice, His Wrath Comes Upon the Wicked, He is Love—and on and on. I could hardly see the print because I got so carried away with my scribbling. Little did I know, my attorney would give the same binder to Jeff during cross-examination and would request that he would turn to the page of my doodling. I thought to myself, Oh my, what have I done—

yikes! Then I had an incredible vision. My scribbling represented "light" and Jeff's lifestyle represented "darkness." Light and darkness collide. Light will always win over darkness. It was as though Jeff could not look down at that page. He kept looking away from it the whole time. I could smell a little victory in the air.

At the end of closing arguments, the judge began rattling off and distributing assets of sixteen years of marriage without much regard. It was quite apparent she was not familiar with the case, as she made careless errors in identifying assets. There was one huge victory and some losses. At this time, I didn't realize how close I came to losing our home. The entire trial culminated in Jeff's attorney pressing that we sell our house and distribute the equity evenly. I later found out Jeff's attorney was also looking out for himself, as his client hadn't paid him. I didn't realize the judge had the power to force me to sell our home. What on earth would I have told my boys? And more importantly, where would we have gone? Thankfully, God gave me the victory and allowed me to keep my house—but with a price. There were lots of stipulations, which gave Jeff nearly 50% of the equity whenever I would sell my home. She also awarded me all of his debt as well. Where was the justice? This man had spent nearly $100,000 of our hard-earned money on an opioid addiction. He even robbed his children's savings accounts. This part of the trial was not justice, but I was then reminded of my recent rebelling. Could this be the consequence for some of my disobedience? Only the good Lord knows the answer. At the end of my trial, a friend reminded me that there is a higher court I can appeal to—God's court, where justice always prevails. She told me not to fear because God will work it out. Well, that's exactly what I'm doing at the present time, eliminating fear. With a lot of prayer, I filed an appeal to the appellate court, where a group of judges would collectively review my case together. I hoped these judges would see the truth and award justice.

December 3, 2003, seemed to last for days. I was blessed to have different neighbors watching my boys after school. When I got home, I collapsed on my bed—drained completely, both emotionally and physically. I remember Thomas offered to cook macaroni for dinner. Thomas and Drew not only took care of themselves at dinner but they showered and put themselves to bed on their own. I think they could sense my weakness. I know I didn't move from the same spot for over six hours. Life had truly been sucked out of me that day. Finally, when midnight rolled around I realized that I should change my clothes and climb into my bed upstairs. I honestly didn't even have the energy to brush my teeth, but at least I was free from oppression.

The next day, I was showered with so much support and love. It was truly a "new" day for me. Trey and Alicia sent me a beautiful arrangement of pink roses with a card that read, "Here's to a New Beginning… We Love You." Wow, that touched me to the core of my soul. Of course, mochas also came in through the front door from neighbors and friends: God's little Valentines. I must have received at least a dozen phone calls that day, from sweet friends who wished me well and gave me words of encouragement. And the emails came flowing in as well. This is what the body of Christ is all about, reaching out to those in need. My whole ordeal has been such a testimony to God. Again, He is the hero in this story!

Well, Christmas 2003 finally came. It was my first Christmas being divorced. I was so thankful that my mother flew in for the holidays to be with my boys and me. Thomas and Drew desperately needed their Grandmother, and I needed the break as well. As soon as my mother walked in the door, she insisted I get out. I did! I went out almost every day during the three weeks she was in town with friends or dates. I stayed very busy. In fact, I stayed too busy. Months later, a friend pointed out that I was probably running away from facing the holidays head-on. I think he was correct in his assumption. If I had slowed down a little, I would have perhaps felt the impact of the holidays.

As the New Year began, I continued meeting and dating a few guys from the Internet. It's funny, single friends understood the concept, whereas married friends didn't. However well-intended, some judged. But most friends were supportive and admitted they wouldn't have a clue what to do either if they were in my shoes. I was appreciative of their honesty. I went into a few relationships here and there, but none seemed right. And I wasn't always obedient to God. Four girlfriends later confessed that they were praying for God to keep all ungodly and wrong men away from me. Things started to become crystal clear, revealing why some relationships ended in mystery. My accountability partner who thought most of the guys from those Internet sites were hot fudge sundaes delivered from Satan! She really didn't think God would bring me my next husband via the Internet. Who knows? When we step out in disobedience, God will allow for heartbreak to occur.

Thankfully, I was strong enough in my walk that I could feel deep convictions from the Holy Spirit. I wasn't that far gone that I couldn't hear God's voice. I was headed in that direction. We as believers are only a few steps away from falling at all times. We are human and we live in these fleshly bodies. But isn't it great that God has given us the gift of His Holy Spirit to keep us on track? It's our decision if we wish to follow. He doesn't and never will force Himself on us. He will never force obedience on us either. However, His rewards are sweet for our obedience. I am humbly grateful to the many family and friends who stood in the gap for me, never giving up on me. I kept falling in some areas but thankfully, Lauren, my accountability partner, never gave up on me nor judged me. She was a faithful friend who never once left my side. She was truly being a sister in Christ to me. By not judging me, our lines of communication and fellowship stayed open. I needed to lean on my friends. Our rebelling is a process that hopefully comes full circle back to Christ.

One day, it hit me like a ton of bricks. God usually speaks to me in the form of scripture, sermon, nature, a word from a friend or song. This time it came through Stacie Orrico's song, "More to Life." I had heard it a hundred times but this dreary, snowy Saturday afternoon in February, I heard this song as though it was the first time. Sitting at a red light, I was moved to tears. She was singing about life. There's got to be more to life than chasing after temporary highs. That's what I was doing. I was trying to control my life instead of allowing God to have control. Surfing these Internet dating sites were my temporary highs. I will quickly say, I don't stand in judgment of others who browse these sites. And actually, some very legitimate dates sites are Christian-based which try to connect people with similar principles. All I knew is that it wasn't God's plan for me. He wanted me to give Him a chance. I needed to be still and hear from Him.

There's got to be more to life than chasing after temporary highs.

Months later, I could step back and see some of the dangers related to these sites. I'm not talking about physical safety, although there's risk in anything we do. Some of these sites are like candy stores for singles. You can pick and choose who you wish to communicate with or get to know better. It's an overload at times. You may start communicating with one person for some time while the other one is still very active in communicating with others on the net. It may not be physical cheating, but it could be emotional cheating depending upon the relationship and the trust that is assumed by both parties. In other words, how does an affair begin in a marriage? It doesn't start with both parties in bed with each other. First, there is an emotional tie that begins to grow stronger if allowed by both parties involved. These are the ingredients of an affair. No one intends for an affair to happen, it just does. I am determined that my second and final marriage will not involve adultery. God gave me a clear vision that some of the people on these sites have the characteristics of committing adultery if married. It all starts with an emotional tie and many don't have the discipline to cut those ties.

As I told many friends who laughed with me, that I was now on a dating hiatus. I meant it! I had had enough of trying it on my own. My plans were not working. I had lots of weaknesses. Perhaps God had better plans! He always does. He's been waiting on the sidelines longing for me to give Him a chance.

CHAPTER 14

An Awakening

"Keep your lives free from the love of money and be content with what you have, because God has said, never will I leave you; never will I forsake you."
— HEBREWS 13:5

IT WAS SPRING 2004, and I was ready for changes in my life; though, I wasn't exactly sure what kind of changes were about to take place. I know I'm thankful the Holy Spirit never would let up on me until I submitted and turned from some rebellious habits. I will forever owe a debt of thanks to the many prayer warriors who never stopped praying for my family and me. I'm not saying I'm safe either, and, I'm not saying I will never fall again into that particular season. But I committed in my heart to be obedient to my Father. It was up to me. Would I be disciplined enough to follow my Father's ways no matter what the costs were, and despite my human weaknesses? I will say I'm not unique. My weaknesses are no different than any other single person. Some may not have identified sin for what it is: sin. I was blinded for a while, so I am the last person to stand in judgment. Unfortunately, I know I will stumble many times in the future. It's a process. The enemy is always standing on the sidelines being your cheerleader, helping you justify your actions. It gets harder to remove those blinders over time simply because your heart has hardened.

I have been a believer ever since I can remember. Actually, I made the decision to give my life to Jesus when I was seven years old. I really didn't have an earth-shattering experience. Let's face it, how many seven-year-olds need to turn from their wicked ways! I was richly blessed to grow up in a home where God was the center. I didn't know any different. Again, this is the richest blessing any parent can give their child. Throughout both my Christian childhood and adulthood, there have been many peaks and valleys along my journey. I tended to walk closer to God when I needed him. And, I tended to push him aside when things were going well. Honestly, those defaults are still in place, which is why it will always be a daily process of dying to self until I draw my last breath.

These last three years have truly been a refining process in my walk. However, over the next few months, my faith continued to grow more than I ever imagined it could. I loved the Lord with all of my heart and soul but never had the intense passion to want Him more than anything else. During this spring season, God crossed my path with a friend who inspired me to take my walk to a higher level. Perhaps God knew John could reach me like nobody else, because of where he was in his season of life. He, too, was a single believer who had a failed marriage with similar circumstances. We had a lot in common as we have walked in very similar shoes, trying to raise kids to know the Lord. We could identify with each other's trials. There are difficult challenges for single parents, but if we relinquish our control to God, then He will guide our steps.

It's an opportunity to trade in the passing pleasures of this world for lasting joy.

I was beginning to experience "Soul Talk" from my friend, which Larry Crabb discusses in his book, *Soul Talk, The Language God Longs for Us to Speak*. This is when we sense the Spirit's rhythm leading us into life-giving, intimate conversations over God. The potential for spiritual growth is then unleashed. We can touch each other's souls in a way that brings growth, meaning, belonging, and great joy. Deeper relationships are products of belonging to God's family. It's an opportunity to trade in the passing pleasures of this world for lasting joy.

The cobwebs were cleared out; thus, my eyes were beginning to focus more clearly on my Father. It's rather difficult to experience the love and joy of real life until we're connected to another at the level of our soul. We cannot know the freedom to be who we truly are until we yield to who we really are to another. I was learning so much about myself during this time. To hear my friend share about his appetite for God and to see it become a ruling passion of his life is inspiring. I have always analyzed most things in my life. Yet, I had never taken time to analyze my faith. Of course, I wanted to stay in the word and know my Father better. But this was on a different field altogether.

My appetite for God was being awakened. When one travels through a season of brokenness, the holy passion lying dormant in the depths of our soul can be released. Perhaps this is the very reason why our Father allows storms to move into our lives. It sometimes takes living a trial of epic proportions until the desire for God becomes a consuming passion of our life. Personally, I was there. I can now fully appreciate and understand what Paul means in James 1: 2-4, *Consider it pure joy whenever you face trials of many kinds, because you know that the testing of your faith develops perseverance. Perseverance must finish its work so that you may be mature and complete, not lacking anything.* I use to almost hate that verse. How could you feel joy when you're in pain? When I was sick with fever for ten months, Trey would lovingly joke about considering my sickness pure joy. What a journey? My sickness developed perseverance in me so that I could handle abandonment. This trial has brought me on a new journey to know God better. A longing and a passion for Him had been ignited. I can finally look back—even in the midst of this painful trial—and say it has been pure joy because my relationship has grown more intimate than I could have ever imagined. Reaching the end of my rope, I realized that self-obsession offers no hope. I also realized that obsession can also be transferred to God. We then give Him a green light to do a mighty work in us. Handcuffing my stubbornness was my biggest battle and challenge. I'm not saying I'm cured either, as yielding will be a daily process for the rest of my life. But we gain tremendous strength and power when we yield which makes submission easier.

When one travels through a season of brokenness, the holy passion lying dormant in the depths of our soul can be released.

The second part of my life was being awakened. God was reaching me, talking to me on the deepest level I've ever experienced. At the beginning of summer in 2004, I found myself flat on my back, recovering from surgery once again. This time around, my doctor experienced some minor complications, which required a fairly good size incision. I was so upset because it meant that the majority of my summer with my boys would be spent recovering from surgery. This seemed so unfair. Lord, haven't I been through enough? I was desperately crying "uncle." Though, God had me once again exactly where He wanted me, dependent upon Him.

Shortly before my surgery, I got into a physical-fitness kick like there was no tomorrow. I was working out in the gym nearly every day and walking about forty miles a week. I couldn't stop nor get enough. It finally occurred to me that I enjoyed this outlet so much because it was the only area I had control of. But most importantly, it was my alone time with God. I felt close to Him as I walked miles every day. I especially enjoyed my walks in the evenings as I watched beautiful sunsets disappear into the landscape over my neighborhood. Sunsets are still my sweet reminders from God, promising to take care of me.

I was so thankful that my mother was able to fly up to Tulsa to take care of Thomas, Drew, and me while I recovered from my surgery. That first week home was a complete blur, as I spent most of the week in bed. However, I can still remember the week after my surgery. It was a Saturday evening and God clearly spoke to me. He told me to get up and go for a walk; He had some things to share with me. There had been many days where I had walked miles and not heard a single word from Him. This night, I was only able to inch myself around a short block in very baby steps. Oh my, God did more talking to me than He ever did during that walk.

Looking back I have to laugh a bit, God probably figured He had my undivided attention as I moved like a feeble senior citizen. I love the comical side of my relationship with my Father because we laugh so much together. Before I rounded the first corner, God was sharing so much with me about my future. I wanted to say, Slow down God, let me get a pen and paper! He began to tell me all is well. He would heal me of ALL my wounds... physically, emotionally, spiritually and financially. He told me that something so great was in store for me and that the latter part of my life would be so wonderful. He went on to say that I was ready for marriage. I said No; I really didn't think I was ready and that I needed time to grow more. God came back in a very firm voice, Daughter, you are ready and I'm preparing my man for you and I will deliver him to you in my perfect timing. I began thinking, Get out of here, no way, God. Are you talking to me?

A major part of me never wants to give my trust away ever again. Who likes rejection? I had such difficulty trusting guys before I was married.

Trusting will be my hardest battle and challenge, as part of me wants to close that door, to never again experience an intimate relationship. But I assume God meant His perfect timing also to teach me that it will be safe to trust again with *His* choice. When I finally finished my walk, I was floored and at the same time, feeling God's perfect peace draped over my body. Then, I came home and wrote down everything He said word-for-word in my journal before I forgot any part of it. And the last thing I said to God before I closed my eyes that night was, God—was all of that stuff you told me tonight true? I could hear Him almost laughing, Trust me, my daughter! Sometimes, I feel like a female "David" in Psalms. I truly speak my mind with God. I'm bellyaching one moment and praising Him the next. He can be a humorous God. Or at least I can say that's a side of Him that He revealed to me many years ago.

My sweet mother ended up staying a total of five weeks helping me. She was such a blessing to our family. It also gave her the opportunity to see how others around "loved on" our family. She was able to see how Thomas and Drew were truly home in this neighborhood. Best friends were everywhere. This was the summer of snakes for them! Many of the boys on our street and my boys hunted garter snakes almost daily behind our house in the woods. For the very first time in all of my life, through the tender innocence of my boys, my fear of snakes began to fade a bit. I did say only a bit. They would name these snakes and then take Sharpie markers and blacken their tails for identification purposes! Weeks later, snakes like Speedy, George, and Clark were found again. Yes, a little humor for Grandma when her darling grandsons would appear at the door with little snakes wrapped around their wrists, just to show off.

My recovery from surgery gave me the opportunity to reflect and set goals. God opened my eyes to new paths He wanted me to take. He was taking me to places I had never been before. For the first time in my walk, God revealed the spiritual gifts He had given me. I probably could have learned this information sooner but this was the first time in my life I was this "still." When you truly "still" your heart, soul, and mind, you begin to hear more from God. My gifts are intercessory prayer and mercy. It finally made perfect sense to me. When you are working so hard in areas in which you are not gifted in, you become burned out and exhausted. When you are working in your gifted areas, you thrive, you grow, and are taken to new heights. You are in your element assisted by the Spirit.

God began to reveal areas I needed to work on with my boys and myself. I begged Him almost daily to be a father to my boys and a husband to me. I had to have His help in raising my boys alone. I knew the enemy wanted a foothold in my boys' lives as he had in so many generations before them with adultery and addictions. Looking at worldly statistics, the odds are stacked against Thomas and Drew because they are coming from a divorced home. I was determined in my heart to fight for my boys; thus, not giving the enemy a foothold in their lives. God, being a husband to me, made it brighter than light I needed to start laying some groundwork. It's going to be hard work but *so* worth the effort.

What kind of legacy did I want to leave Thomas and Drew? I wanted to instill in them the same passion I had to know our Father better. I knew in my heart the only way to accomplish that desire was to lead by example. And if I was to lead by example, then I needed to grow more and be disciplined. The only way to grow more is to spend more time with God. I thought to myself, How in the world would I find more time? I was already running ragged. Oh my, when you voice your desire to God wanting to know Him better, He will make your path straight. He will show you lots of ways. You just need to be "still" long enough to hear from Him.

I don't know if you are like me but I'm guilty of spending too many hours on the computer. It seems as though that our computers have replaced the television remote. I sit at my computer all day long doing work. I have realized that I spent a great deal of my free time surfing the Internet. I use to spend hours checking and writing emails, instant messaging, surfing sites anywhere from medical billing, business, or cooking, to news outlets. What if I exchanged that time for God and my family? Would my family benefit? Would I benefit? The answer is yes, the next answer is yes and the last answer is yes! Do you get my point? Our lives began to change more when I directed my extra time from the computer to God and my family. I also found much needed time for myself. I think our society has grown a bit lazy with computers. You don't have to pick up the phone to hear a friend's voice; you can email or text them. It's quicker and easier; though, very impersonal. I think sometimes we are missing out on the big picture by not connecting with others.

I started changing the way I did things around home. I started having a Bible study with Thomas and Drew before bedtime. How else would they learn how to have a quiet time? I can't expect the church to teach them. It needs to come from example in the home. The greatest joys I now experience is when Drew will come up to me at night with their Boys' Bible study book in hand and tell me it's time for Bible Study. I know God must be smiling.

Another area I began changing in my life was cooking with my boys. It was a passion of mine before these trials. There's a huge part of me that is old fashioned. I was beginning to rediscover the real me. I love cooking for my family and I thought why not share this passion with my boys. It's part of who I am and how God made me. Perhaps one day their wives will thank me because my boys will know how to do more than boil water in the kitchen! Even Drew has learned how to sauté onions and peppers. Thomas has also broadened his cooking skills from macaroni and cheese to hamburgers and much more. We started doing that old fashion tradition of eating dinner together rather than in shifts.

It's true what they say, you can learn so much from your children over dinner. Turn off all noises and really listen to them. We even started dining outside under the stars, which has been fun for them and sweet for me. Through this process, I have learned so much more about my boys and the young men they are becoming. It's been a matter of taking time and "smelling the roses." There was a period during this trial where my focus was on unnecessary extracurricular activities. In the grand scheme of things, these things did not matter. I had to trust God and know that He would meet all of my needs. I had to let go of junk. In exchange, I have found myself not only falling more in love with God but with my boys. My relationship with Thomas and Drew has grown much deeper. We must not take for granted nor forget families are treasures from God.

—

CHAPTER 15

A Season for Rebuilding

"For everyone born of God overcomes the world. This is the victory that has overcome the world, even our faith."
— 1 John 5:4

Our family was slowly falling into a routine of becoming a family again. Summer had been a time for redecorating my soul. August was filled with lots of little getaways before school started. We were playing catch-up since I spent the majority of our summer recovering from my surgery. Once again, we were blessed with Fingerprints for friends who invited our family up to the lake on several occasions. Another family gave my boys and me a trip to Silver Dollar City in Branson, Missouri to have one last summer fling before school started. It was a trip I thoroughly enjoyed because it was just Thomas, Drew and me. We hit the water parks together as well as the roller coasters from sunup to sundown. It was nice to see them smiling a lot. Our family is beginning to be rich in spirit again.

Two days after school had started, it was Friday the 13th¯my 41st birthday! I mention this day only because it was the beginning of something new for me. I was experiencing a new and unfamiliar feeling; I began to recognize this feeling as true joy. Three of my nearest and dearest friends had taken me to lunch at my favorite restaurant in Utica Square—a collection of neat, trendy upscale shops and restaurants in midtown. The sidewalks have beautiful landscaping with large trees everywhere that form canopies throughout Utica Square.

August was unseasonably cool including the day of my birthday. My friends and I sat outside and had nearly a three-hour lunch soaking up our surroundings. The birds were singing. Every half hour, the clock's chimes would play soothing sounds that seemed to come off the pages of a fairy tale. It was so tranquil. I cannot ever remember having a lunch lasting that long without once looking down at my watch. For that moment—time didn't matter and the company of my friends was priceless. It was the best lunch I had in my life. You're reading about another Fingerprint, a birthday gift of deep, inner peace from God. This was a depth of joy I have never known before.

Two weeks later, I was blessed with a long, relaxing weekend with friends. It was a weekend of regrouping and a time to recharge my batteries of being a single Mom. It has changed my life and the way I look at life. It was the first signal I received from God that this was the beginning phase that would end my trial. It was a girls' weekend getaway deep down in the heart of Texas with my three best friends. They made the arrangements. I don't remember a time where I was able to momentarily escape the pressures and responsibilities of being a mother and provider. I once again felt a sensational feeling of real joy that's impossible to describe. The beauty of friendship was brighter than light. It wasn't about anything we did, but rather, it was about what God did for us.

One of our outings was a float trip down the Guadalupe River. Even though our float trip lasted for many hours, time appeared to stand still, thus granting us the privilege of taking in our scenic surroundings. Natural beauty, which I use to take for granted, seemed to jump off the page. I felt like a little kid on an adventure. I remember floating a great deal of the time with my eyes closed, listening to the river with an occasional "heads-up" shout from my friends. (A warning to pick my head up off of my float before colliding with a boulder!) We were enjoying the tranquility the river offered.

Again, God was showing me this new feeling I was beginning to recognize as joy. Would I experience this joy if it were not for the heartbreak I had endured over the last three years? Probably not. I learned there is a real difference between happiness and joy. The two are not the same. I once read that happy people are unable to know love like joyful people. I had a hard time understanding that particular concept, but now I understand. Happy people are typically very content with what they have and feel blessed. They are willing to help others in need, but their primary focus is often in keeping what they have. In order to pursue a greater and bigger dream, they must be freed. This is the reason why there's a limit to their love. In His severe mercy, God removes the good to cause a longing for the better things. As a result, He satisfies a new craving, thus enabling and liberating us to love more deeply. Enduring long periods of difficulty causes one to appreciate the simple things.

Often, we may long for better days until the rug is pulled out from underneath. It is only then you realize just how much treasure you held in your hands. A new appreciation for the simple life you once had begins to emerge from the inner depths of your soul. This is exactly why I can praise my Father for my sufferings, because the inner depths of my soul may have never been unlocked. I honestly didn't believe I would ever have this incredible passion to want my Father more than anything else in this life. I wish everyone could feel this way. Wouldn't our world be a better place to live? But we must remember that this place is just our temporary home. God doesn't want us getting too comfortable here as He has paradise waiting for us on the other side.

In His severe mercy, God removes the good to cause a longing for the better things.

My furnace has been hot for much longer than I wish! During this trial, I have grabbed a hold of so many stories in the Old Testament for hope. I am thankful for the trials Job endured a few thousand years ago so that today, his very distant relatives, like me, can benefit from his story. I love the story in Daniel when Shadrach, Meshach, and Abednego refused to worship King Nebuchadnezzar's idol. Our idols today can be anything from over indulging in food, shopping, acquiring material possessions, the desire for prestige, too much time on the Internet, sex, alcohol, sports—and of course, opioids. Idols can be anything that becomes a stronghold and takes our focus off of God. Don't get me wrong, I love shopping, sports, and desserts, but there are limits before these things consume us.

Shadrach, Meshach, and Abednego didn't do what the world expected them to do. They were in the minority and took a stand in their faith for God. Man, did they ever go on a faith walk! My hope and prayer for my family is based upon this story. My boys and I have been through the furnace because of opioids. I wouldn't wish this kind of trial on anyone. At times, I'm surprised that it hasn't broken us, but we have a supernatural strength dwelling within us. It's not about us. My hope is that Thomas,

Drew, and I will rise out of this fiery furnace refined and polished without the smell of smoke or any evidence of soot on us. What a testimony it's going to be to our Maker and Creator! My boys will hopefully have a deeper appreciation for life as adults.

As stated in Isaiah, it's darkest before dawn. How true! As I've started feeling evidence that dawn is really peaking behind the clouds, I hit rock-bottom in an area of my life that's been difficult to talk about from the very beginning. But God has grown me in the area of my finances. Once again, my Father has me exactly where He wants me in the final season of this trial.

We all go through life with our dreams, where we want to be and where we don't want to be. As I mentioned earlier, it often takes brokenness to gain a greater appreciation of what was there. Looking back to the days shortly after my college graduation, I had many hopes and dreams for my future. I would have never dreamed in a million years my life would have taken this radical of a turn. I thought if ever I got divorced and had to start dating again, I would just die. Well, newsflash! At the young age of 41, I'm still around and in probably better shape than I've ever been in my life. The rock-bottom in my finances that I hit last month was never on the radar screen. In other words, I never imagined what would happen if I needed that kind of help. Help was just never an option because my life would never travel down that road. Wrong! My journey brought me to a juncture that I was never programmed to take in life. It's been a humbling experience, to say the least.

If all of this had occurred last year, I would have lost it—curled up and disappeared paralyzed with pain. Yeah, God knows exactly what we can handle! But what is so amazingly cool is that I have a joy in my heart that has brought me out of the boat to Jesus. It is really OK because He is in charge of my life. One by one, His promises to me are being delivered as the stormy seas are beginning to settle down. If God gives you a word, a vision or a dream, then *bank on it.*

This reminds me of the morning of my divorce trial when I woke up and wasn't sure exactly where to turn in the Bible to have my quiet time. I just said, God, bring me to a place where you can reach me. When I opened my Bible, it opened up to the last chapter in Job. I remember I had this great big smile on my face and I looked up and said, You are funny God! I smiled because of what my small group leader told me a few weeks earlier. I had been so heartbroken because Jeff had emptied most of our hard-earned savings and left me with a ton of his debt. What on earth was I going to do? How was I going to start over at the age of 40? Kathy came back and said, Silly, look at Job… he got it all back and then some! I could hear God telling me the same thing as He brought me to the last chapter of Job on the morning of my trial. He is faithful and He is a God of justice.

A healthy and reverend respect for fear of God is something I have gained over the last few months. Perhaps the most important lesson God has wanted to teach me all along. I wasn't paying attention. I've always had an open relationship with God since I was a child. Meaning, I've never feared Him. I look at Him like my Daddy but on a supernatural scale. Maybe that explains why I freely sinned in some areas of my life because I wasn't afraid of the consequences.

As a child, I could do no wrong. After all, God would forgive me. I thought the way I worshipped God was fine. For the longest time during this trial, I could only see my pain, not God. I thought I saw God but was deceived with these blinders that we as humans wear. I kept thinking God would deliver me. I've got to have hope, that's what the scripture says. I've always been an optimistic person who prefers to see the glass as half-full rather than half-empty. I didn't realize that I was subconsciously thinking in a way of being in control until a few weeks had passed. Both faith and trust are unseen. We are taught from the Word that obedience and faithfulness produces rewards and deliverance. This is all very true. Over time, however, I allowed my thinking to bring me to a point where God owed me deliverance from this trial. God doesn't owe us a thing. He is a good God because He loves us so much and He longs to give us the desires of our heart. I was beginning to hear my heart speak. I mean really *speak*, on a deeper and intimate level. I never knew this part of my heart existed! I don't deserve God's blessings, but it is in His nature to bless his children. I was crying out telling God to do as He wished with me. God, show me how I can fulfill your dreams. I am now trusting Him on a level I've never experienced before in my life. This is the joy I was describing earlier in this chapter. Lately, when I'm all alone, I find myself smiling more and more. Life is good because God blesses each of us every day with a new hope! He is all the strength I will ever need, as He will carry me through the valleys.

CHAPTER 16

A New Sunrise

"Now to him who is able to do immeasurably more than all we ask or imagine, according to his power that is at work within us"

— Ephesians 3:20

I love to see sunrises in October. There is something about how the sunrays twinkle through the trees. The leaves are just beginning to fall and change colors. It's a sign that not only winter but the holidays are around the corner—one of my favorite times of the year. I love the cool crisp weather, also known as *football weather* in most parts of the country. There's nothing better than watching college football games on a cold Saturday afternoon. I also love going on brisk walks this time of the year—traversing the leaf-covered sidewalks. And, I always love burying my boys in piles of leaves. Who doesn't?

October is also the month my Daddy went home to be with the Lord, many years ago. This particular year on the anniversary of his death, I was traveling with friends and family to Branson, Missouri. The many shades of color illuminating off the Ozark Mountains were breathtaking. It's really hard to describe in words just how beautiful the colors were on that autumn day. Any adjectives would not do it justice. God brought a smile to my heart on this day as I remembered Daddy. I still miss him dearly and often wonder what he would think of my life today. I sometimes think it really is a blessing that he is not here to witness what has happened to his little girl. He would have been so heartbroken. Though, I would like to think he would be smiling about now saying, Well done my, daughter. I'm thinking what a special Fingerprint from God that He is lifting me out of this trial during a favorite time of the year.

When I began writing this book, I had no idea where my life would be headed. I simply didn't have any control over my future. God woke me up in the middle of the night almost two years ago and He planted a vision in me. He wanted my boys to have a memorial of this season in our family's life. God gave me a picture of the memorial He instructed Joshua to erect in Joshua 4 at Gilgal. A memorial can be seen generations after what transpired before. With regards to Thomas and Drew, there has been so much that has happened and will happen that is above their comprehension. In other words, they don't have enough maturity in their sweet, innocent years to understand the ugliness of an opioid crisis that resulted in my divorce with their father. When they become adults, they need to know what God did for our family. They need to know about the mountains God moved on our behalf. But the vision God revealed to me early one winter morning has proven to be a vision with unlimited blessings. Isn't this just like God? When we follow Him, He always seems to knock our socks off beyond what any of us can fathom, which reminds me of Ephesians 3:20: *He can do immeasurably more than we can imagine!* The art of healing has been the other blessing from this vision.

Initially, it took several months before I actually started writing about all of this. I wrote in small segments but stopped for long periods because it was too painful to re-live those difficult moments. Thc byproducts of addiction are brutal—all of it affected my precious family. God relentlessly stayed on me until I started writing again. Perhaps I was doing exactly what many people do, as I discussed in earlier chapters regarding counseling and therapy. I was burying the pain by not writing; hence, I didn't have to feel. Who wants to feel pain? In these fleshly bodies that we live in, we always think we know what's best for us, right? Thankfully, God always knows what's in our best interest. Thankfully, He really *is* in control. This reminds me of a parent trying to give their children nasty-tasting medicine. Some children will practically do anything to avoid taking medicine, but of course, the parent will not give in because they know the medication

The byproducts of addiction are brutal—all of it affected my precious family.

is necessary for healing. Our Father is no different; He knows what is necessary for our well-being.

I strongly feel my Father will use His vision through this book to reach others experiencing dark hours. He wants to give all of His children hope in their lives. Our society is so twisted today. We don't have a clue what it is like to be patient. Patience almost sounds like a foreign term. We want instant gratification; thus, many things gained don't have the value of appreciation. Do we even know what being still means anymore?

As I'm beginning to see glimpses of dawn, I'm starting to taste something I've been searching for years to experience. It is true, genuine freedom! This is where my Father has wanted me all along. He wants me to be totally and completely satisfied in Him. It's a place I had to come to all on my own. For some of us, like myself, it might take heartbreak or a tragedy to get here. Nobody could do it for me. Sometimes, pain is the only way for God to get our attention.

All of my life, without even knowing it, I've been dependent on others for a certain degree of my needs. As a child, I depended on my parents for security, stability, consistency, and emotional support. Then, when I graduated from high school, I left home for college. Still, I was dependent on my parents. From singlehood, I moved into the covenant of marriage. My husband met many of those same needs. He was my best friend, a father to our children, and a provider. Again, I was dependent on someone else other than God. Never in my life had I really stood on my own. I've always had somebody else to lean on which has truly blocked my inability to rely solely on God.

For the first time, I've allowed God to be my "everything." He is the boss of my life. He is in control. Hence, I have finally understood what it means to be set free! I can honestly admit I don't need anyone else to make me happy. That's a big statement for me! I want God more than anything else in this world. I can now identify with a passage Paul talks about in 1 Corinthians 7 that it is good to stay unmarried. In this season, it's been just God and me. I strongly feel my relationship with my Father would not have grown this much with someone else in my life. I am so thankful I halted dating for a while. Besides, He has better plans for me. I needed the time to meditate and be pure before my Father. Time with someone else would have robbed my alone time with God. It would have been a distraction from my growth process. Yet, I understand there is strength in unity with your soulmate but I want my foundational relationship rock solid before I meet someone. I want to offer God's very best.

Some people view being single as a lonely time in their life. I get that; I've been there and I understand. For example, there used to be a time in my life where Saturday evenings were lonely in my neighborhood. The landscape outside screamed *families* and it made me feel vulnerable that we did not have a complete family. Driving up to church on Sunday mornings, seeing cars filled with families again reminded me my family was not whole. I'm quite sure nobody else saw us that way, but I did. That was the enemy trying to steal my joy. I allowed God to deliver me from those feelings of inadequacy last spring. I have never had a thought of inadequacy since, and I praise my Father for that spirit of confidence and wholeness that only He can fill. In other words, my Father completes my family.

I view this season of being single as an opportunity for spiritual growth. I would encourage all single people to take advantage of the solitude without the responsibilities of commitment to someone else. Grow yourself to be the best Godly spouse if that is the direction your Father takes you on. Like anything that is worth the effort, it takes discipline and stillness. These are characteristics our society lacks today. So often, we miss God's blessings because we step ahead of Him. Patience is all about numbers. Patience is the willingness to wait for God's plan. Patience is giving up on instant gratification. He's never made a mistake. Every time I've stepped out on my own will, I have failed miserably. For me, it takes discipline in all areas; it's practicing being controlled by the spirit rather than the flesh.

So many times, I've wanted desperately to give into my desires rather than wait on God. I still struggle today and will always struggle on this side. I am thankful God has given us His supernatural word in the form of the Bible. Our distant Biblical relatives did not endure hardships for nothing. God allowed all of the historical events written in the Bible for us today. Surely we can learn from the rebellious Israelites not to make the same mistakes but for some reason we still do today. And the consequences are still the same. I wonder why I am still so strong-willed at times. However, I've learned that I'm stronger through my weaknesses.

What is so cool and hard to describe in words is the ever-evolving journey Christ will take us on. He is such a mystery. Just when I think I have God figured out is when I realize how little I know about Him. Last year at this time, I thought I had a great walk with God. Today, it is better than it was yesterday. God will continually reveal more of Himself to you as He takes you deeper into knowing Him. If we are not growing in Him, then we are sliding away from Him. The more He reveals Himself to me, the more passionately I want to know Him better.

I have now marked my one-year anniversary of being divorced. Ann told me the evening of my trial: Remember this moment in time and use it as a measure for next year and the year after. In other words, it would help measure my healing and growth. Just two short years ago, my life seemed almost hopeless. I wanted to go to sleep and not wake up. The daily pain was almost too difficult to bear, but by the grace of God, I survived those dark hours.

Now, I am experiencing more joy than I have in years, perhaps ever. I feel a deep peace within my soul. My attitude has changed so much even as recent as this past summer. I see more when my eyes are closed.

Through this whole trial, God has truly blessed me with sweet slumber. It's a blessing that not many have regardless of trials or no trials. So many people suffer from insomnia. But my Father has given me the priceless treasure of uninterrupted sweet rest. In other words, I don't have that long after my head hits the pillow to think about things before I'm out. Sometimes, I like to rewind my day and look for God's Fingerprints. However, this past week, God revealed to me another area marking progress in my healing. I realized that most of this last week, I have giggled myself to sleep thinking of the funny things that He's shown me. You may wonder what the significance of this means. It is another confirmation from God that I am Free; it is another confirmation that I am healing. I have never giggled myself to sleep before probably because I have always had so much going on in my life. I have always tried to shoulder the burden with God. Every night when I go to sleep, I tell God to take all of my burdens. It's His battle, not mine. Besides, He wants full control of our battles. Wow, what love He has for us! What a Father, wanting to take care of all of the crud in our lives.

Another area in my life that God has really worked on is forgiveness. It's obvious how my ex-husband wounded me the most. He allowed the enemy a foothold into our lives, which destroyed our marriage, a sacred covenant with God, which I took seriously. Now I've come full circle and the anger I once had for my ex-husband is almost non-existent. It's not my battle as God is my avenger. He is a God of justice and I know without a shadow of doubt, my family will be served justice. My appeal is with God's court and I've let go. Though, it tends to hurt more when brothers and sisters in Christ hurt us. But we're all human. However, as brothers and sisters in Christ, we are held accountable and held to a higher standard. We are not of this world.

They say you lose friends in a divorce. I am thankful this has not been the case for me, with the exception of a handful of families. I think the only reason a few friends have distanced themselves from us (or anyone else who has gone through a divorce) is because they are uncomfortable with our circumstances. Our dance has changed. As Janet would always tell me… these friends would prefer the way things used to be; therefore, our current circumstances are uncomfortable for them. When someone has cancer, typically the innermost being of a person desires to reach out to that person and show compassion. However, why does our society treat a person who is divorced with distance rather than with compassion?

Like with some forms of cancer, divorce is a form of death. Divorce is a death of a marriage, death of a family, death of dreams never to be realized. Our former life as we knew it is gone. We are not those people anymore. I'd like to think we have been refined and have so much more to offer. However, I have gained a supernatural amount of wonderful friends. I am blessed. What I have learned and gained through the experience of divorce and the advice I would share is to reach out to those who are hurting. Even if you don't know what to say, your presence and support speaks volumes. Abandonment, silence or distance speaks rejection. In other words, don't dissolve relationships when they are already down. Take up the cross and stand in the gap for your family or friends. It's that simple and there's no scientific formula. There are eternal rewards for ministering to ones in need. It's all part of being the body of Christ and uniting together for strength.

Our lives are filled with many blessings as well as shattered dreams. It is up to us how we will walk through life… with or without God. Will we walk with dignity and grace or with bitterness? Will we have enough strength and discipline to trust God?

I have recently discovered God's secret of abundant life! Actually, it's not a secret. It's not about success, health, or family. Rather, it's about knowing our Father intimately. I cannot adequately describe in words this relationship. Words would do no justice in describing God; they would make Him smaller than He really is. Though, I can now say that not only do I love God but I'm in love with Him. He is a beautiful mystery, which will be revealed on the other side of our journey. Just know the deeper we grow in Him, the more He will bless us with His abundant life. He doesn't owe us a thing; though, He desires to shower us with blessings. If He gives you a word, then have the patience to wait on Him.

This summer on one of my evening walks, He made it brighter than light. I believe He was preparing His choice for a spouse for me. He has never misled me with the wrong information. I look at this waiting period as an opportunity to share with my boys through example of meeting your future mate. I have such an important role in their young lives, regardless if I'm divorced or not. I can lead through example; I can teach them how to respect women. I can attempt to teach them the right way to be in their future relationships.

There's an important movement in many church youth groups throughout our nation called True Love Waits. It teaches our youth about abstinence and being pure before God. This program shares with youth about the beauty of being intimate with your spouse, and the boundaries God created sex for which is marriage. I think if parents would take the time to really share how beautiful the treasure their children have in keeping themselves pure, then perhaps singles would be more eager to wait on God. How will they know how beautiful it can be if we as parents don't share with them?

Unfortunately, there are too many single, Christian adults as well who believe they are immune to this particular principle God has set for His children. What a wonderful opportunity for single parents to teach their children that true love really does wait. If Mom or Dad can be pure before God, then maybe it will be easier for children to follow the examples of their parents.

As a child, I always heard my Grandmother say, "Honey, you need to start praying for God to give you a wonderful husband one day." I believed the truth in what she said, but I never really practiced it, as my walk was weak in my youth. Now, I have so much more at stake this time around. I have two important and precious sons in my life. I have to have God's guidance. Actually, I have absolutely no desire to pick my next and final mate. God has to do it and as I've often joked, God will have to deliver him on my front door step standing on a silver platter. A yellow sticky affixed to his head that states "I am from God" would help, too! I feel it is important to write about this, as I know there are many other single parents in my shoes. This is critical. There is no time for guessing games. There's a song that came out a few years ago that plays in my head at times. I mentioned in previous chapters, how God often speaks to my heart through songs. The song "Wait for me" by Rebecca St. James is no exception.

Wait for Me
By Rebecca St. James

Darling, did you know that I
I dream about you
Waiting for the look in your eyes
When we meet for the first time
Darling, did you know that I
I pray about you
Praying that you will hold on
And keep your loving eyes only for me

Cause I am waiting for
Waiting for you, darling
Wait for me too
Wait for me as I wait for you
Cause I am waiting for
Waiting for you darling
Wait for me too
Wait for me as I wait for you
Darling,wait

Darling did you know I dream about life together
Know you'll be forever
I'll be yours and you'll be mine
And darling when I say
Til death do us part
I'll mean it with all of my heart
Now and always faithful to you

Cause I am waiting for
Waiting for you darling
Wait for me too
Wait for me as I wait for you
Cause I am waiting for
Waiting for you darling
Wait for me too
Wait for me as I wait for you
Darling, wait
Darling, wait

Now I know you have made mistakes
But there's forgiveness and a second chance
So wait for me darling
Wait for me
Wait for me
Wait for me

Cause I am waiting for
Waiting for you, darling
Wait for me, too
Wait for me as I wait for you
Cause I am waiting for
Waiting for you, darling
Wait for me too
Wait for me as I wait for you
Darling, wait.....

It's a beautiful serenade. Wouldn't it be beautiful to tell your spouse they were worth the wait? And wow, can you imagine the beautiful and indescribable blessings God would bestow on your marriage. Since I'm older this time around, I've heard many stories from other divorced singles that "waited" for their second marriage. Every single story has the same happy ending: The second marriage is so much better than the first. They didn't have to go looking for their spouse; God brought them together just as He brought Eve to Adam in the garden. That's nothing less than God's perfect hand. He is capable of what seems like the impossible. Give Him a chance. Allow Him to work in the many blessings He has given you as well as the shattered dreams He has allowed to enter into your life.

I have survived the darkest hours of my life and I am anxiously looking forward to my future journey. God is in control and I'm excited! My deepest desire is to leave a legacy to my sons of knowing God better. When others are in Thomas and Drew's presence, I hope they will be able to see God's reflection. Life is unfolding exactly as it needs to for me. And so, all is well with my soul.

CHAPTER 17

Going Home

"Every good and perfect gift is from above, coming down from the Father of the heavenly lights, who does not change like shifting shadows."

— James 1:17

I love the way God often reminds me He is in control. Take this book for example; He woke me up in the middle of the night a few years ago to write this, to record our testimony as a memorial to my darling sons, Thomas and Drew. The same applied to Joshua and the Israelites. At Gilgal, the entrance of the Promised Land, the Lord instructed Joshua to lead the Israelites to set up twelve stones to serve as a memorial. These stones were to serve as a memorial for generations to come, as proof of God leading His children out of Egypt into the Promised Land. God wants us to be reminded of His great works. He doesn't want us to forget His faithfulness.

In my small mind, I thought the previous chapter in this book would be my last. I was at peace in this season of my life. I cannot find accurate words to describe this peace other than to say that it's supernatural. Well, as always, God had other plans for me! I don't know about you, but it never fails; God's plans for me always turn out far different than I could ever plan. I was looking forward to the upcoming year. Though, I had no idea my Father was getting ready to take me on the ride of my life.

It was Christmas, 2004. Two years had now passed since our world had been shaken off the Richter scale. By my measure, it was the hardest two years of my life and the most painful years in my boys' young lives.

Yet, we were still standing by the grace of God. The boys and I had not been home to Louisiana since that time. I just didn't have it in me to face family and friends. I didn't feel like explaining my life nor did I want to face any kind of judgment. It was so surreal, almost deja vu. God was up to something. He had a plan. It was time to close chapters once and for all so that new ones could be unveiled. I never imagined closing emotional and mental chapters would take physical efforts on my part—like a long trip back home.

Two years earlier, the boys and I went down to Louisiana the week before Christmas to celebrate my nephew's wedding. Drew was in the wedding. You read about it in earlier chapters. At that time, we were an intact family. Exactly two years later, it was time to celebrate my other nephew's wedding. This time, both Thomas and Drew were in the wedding. All of the wedding guests, including us, stayed at the same hotel. However, it was a different year, different brother, different wedding, but the same family. I even borrowed my neighbor's same suitcase like I did two years earlier. In a weird and funky way, it felt creepy—because everything was the same. It's like God was giving us a do-over.

A few days before I left, I had to go see Janet and run all of this by her. She agreed that all of the upcoming events were of no coincidence. She suggested I journal daily while on my visit, and to be still so I could hear from God. We both agreed that He was up to something!

Of course, I was a bit apprehensive about my visit. Except for my mother and brother, nobody down there had seen me since I was divorced. When one goes through a divorce, there are a million feelings you experience. Rejection and self-esteem issues are good for starters. You believe that family and friends will treat you the same—some do and some don't. However, that's exactly how the enemy wants you, fearful. Thankfully, my eyes had been firmly planted on my Heavenly Father. I was safe in His arms.

I will say it was the most relaxed visit I've ever had in the fourteen years since I moved away from Louisiana. Thomas and Drew enjoyed being with family. They were in desperate need of being loved on by family. They craved the attention, especially by male members who were available for them. This reminded me of stories from the Bible. When there was a death or the father became absent, the brothers stepped in his place to fill in the gap. Thomas and Drew enjoyed the opportunity to spend time with their uncles.

Little did I know at the time, chapters were being closed. It is hard to understand unless you've been there. It was the afternoon of December 21, 2004, I was all alone in my childhood home for a few hours while my mother had taken Thomas and Drew into town. God told me to get up and read His Word. For the last few weeks, I had spent my quiet time in Genesis. The next chapter in Genesis was 24. This was the very first time God gave me a glimpse that He was going to deliver my husband on a silver platter.

Ok, you might chuckle at that last statement! But seriously, He did give me a vision. Genesis 24 talks about Abraham sending his servant out to his homeland to find a wife for Isaac. On the servant's journey to find Isaac's wife, he brought his master's camels and all kinds of gifts to present to Isaac's future bride and her family. He was on a specific mission, bearing gifts. And, as Abraham's servant neared his hometown, the servant began to pray a specific prayer that he would know exactly who Isaac's future bride would be without any question. Before he finished praying, Rebekah was standing in front of him. Have you gotten any goosebumps yet? I have!

Through these passages, God told me He would deliver my husband on a silver platter and that I would know without a shadow of doubt who my husband would be when He crossed my path with his. I thought, Ok Lord, I don't know how this will take place or happen but I trust you. I figured Ok, you're the Master of the Universe, surely you can play "cupid" on a supernatural level. Playing matchmaker for one child has to be a piece of cake compared to other miracles like parting the Red Sea or talking the world into existence, don't you agree?

As I finished reading Genesis 24, realizing He was giving me a vision of my future, I looked up and noticed the most beautiful sunset. In fact, it occurred to me that the location where I was viewing this fabulous work of art was the very place I first fell in love with sunsets. It was on our family farm in South Louisiana. When I was a child, I can remember stopping in awe many afternoons to look across the highway and across the fields to view spectacular sunsets. It hit me right then and there, Candy, this is why you love sunsets so much. I saw hundreds of them as a child. Going home opened my eyes up to why simple sunsets were deeply rooted in my spirit.

As a child, God was preparing me as He painted beautiful sunsets to use them as an avenue to speak to me as an adult. I remember I was almost mesmerized that cold December afternoon staring at His beautiful work. Again, I cannot explain it in words other than saying I felt "safe."

When I journey back down to the heart of Cajun country, I make it a point to eat all of my favorites and have a deep connection with these places. Each day of my visit, I discovered more things about myself. It's as though I was able to view my life from a different perspective. God had me on this incredible journey. From the moment we are born, He knows what is going to unfold in our lives. He had to take me back to my roots to open new doors in this season of my life.

When I came back home to Oklahoma, I was forever changed. I cannot explain it, even as I'm writing this chapter two years later. Something happened to me. I was truly excited about life. Yes, there was still plenty of uncertainty in my life, but God's grace was sufficient. I think I could finally identify with the passages in 2 Corinthians 12:7-10 ,when Paul pleads with God to remove the thorn from his side. And God comes back to Paul and says, "My grace is sufficient for you." Wow! When life begins to crumble, when everything appears to be out of control, only then can God's unsurpassable peace calm you and give you the assurance to go on. There was no way I could have held on without His perfect peace. Things were still out of my control, but then again, isn't that the way He prefers it? In other words, I was still reminded that *He* was in control. A very difficult lesson I've had to learn over and over.

When life begins to crumble, when everything appears to be out of control, only then can God's unsurpassable peace calm you and give you the assurance to go on.

CHAPTER 18

Healing Rain

"For I am the Lord your God who takes hold of your right hand and says to you, Do not fear; I will help you."
— Isaiah 41:13

This chapter begins with a New Year, 2005. I can remember only two short years ago, how this New Year began with much pain and uncertainty. Life was raw. Life was so close to being hopeless for me.

Jeff had just left our family. I was in a dense fog and didn't have a clue how we were going to survive. It seemed like it lasted a lifetime. But in reality, it was only two years and now, it seems like a lifetime ago. My God never left my side. The refining process has been indescribable. Although I couldn't see daylight, the storm was beginning to lift. I could see God's faithful hand at work. The path of destruction caused by my now-ex-husband's opioid addiction would become a distant memory. Looking back in the rearview mirror, I think of all of the lessons I have learned while overcoming the impossible. I never dreamed God would give me the strength to overcome—but He did!

During many of my quiet times with the Lord, I felt, deep down in my Spirit, that God was doing reconstructive work on my heart. (And isn't there always construction work going on?) He was doing some major renovations in my life. I didn't know what, how, or where, but I could just sense something was coming. As I write this, God is connecting a few dots for me as He's done in previous chapters. His Fingerprints are everywhere. I can now look back and see how God laid the groundwork. Little events, happenings, or meetings occur for a reason. We may not see it then or ever but nothing in life happens by coincidence. I'm always telling my family there is no such thing as luck. God is always in control. There are no ifs, ands or buts about His presence or power.

Remember in earlier chapters Jeff had this incredible group of male friends? These guys formed a small group called Iron Man. They did Life together by encouraging one another. They reached out in so many ways to help Jeff during those early days. They were wonderful to our family. I knew the guys but never really had the opportunity to get to know any of their wives except Kristie. I firmly believe Kristie was planted in the beginning to help me in that initial season after Jeff left us. I was getting ready to have the opportunity to know more of the wives.

Shortly after New Year's, Ed invited the boys and me to join their family for lunch after church. The previous month, I had been over to their home for a meal making party hosted by Ed's wife, Sarah. Sarah had been a Homemade Gourmet consultant for several years.

Little did I know that lunch was going to change our lives forever! I am not kidding! I will begin to connect the dots as God takes our family on this incredible journey in 2005. As I'm writing this book two years later, God is opening my eyes and giving me glimpses of how He plays the role of Cupid. I couldn't see it then but now it's obvious how He had so many things fall into place before He made His first move. God is so much bigger than we will ever fathom on this side of eternity. Don't ever think you will have God figured out! You won't. Don't ever think you can put God in a box. It's not possible.

Prior to Jeff leaving, I use to love showing hospitality to friends in our home. Two weeks after having lunch with Sarah and Ed, Sarah contacted me wanting to discuss Homemade Gourmet. She wanted to know if I would be interested in becoming a consultant hosting meal-making parties. I told her I hated anything relating to sales. She mentioned I could host only the parties for now. So, I went home to think and pray about it for a long time. She suggested it would be a great way to earn extra income.

Since Jeff was not providing child support, it was painfully difficult attempting to make ends meet every month for my family. I began to hear God telling me to go for it. I thought, No way Lord I hate sales. Then, I could hear His small quiet voice, "Candy, are you going to trust me?" Ok Lord, I said, "I've taken some very big leaps of faith these last two years and every time, you have come through!" So, I put my name on the dotted line and officially became a consultant. It took some time but I started preparing for these monthly parties. With enough planning, I was hoping to have my first party in April. I figured it would be as good a time as any. Any delays on my part would constitute as caving into fear.

As my life took on a new direction, I was beginning to feel His tugging at me to start a small group for ladies. With my recent, real-life experiences, my compassion for single moms/ladies began to deepen. I didn't know if God wanted to use me to help other women who had been through similar circumstances or not. I didn't have any of the answers yet. There was some excitement in the air but still lots of uncertainty. Before divorce, I use to be the type of individual who had to be in control and know everything that was going on. You think He changed me in that area? You bet.

I was eager to see what God was going to do with a new small group, but at the same time, I felt like I was leaving home, too. Over the last three years, my small group became my family. They stood in the gap for me and held my hand tightly for those years. The support they provided would take many books to write about. Thomas and Drew felt such a connection with my small group. It became their family as well. Each member touched us in many ways. I would have to spend several lifetimes repaying them for what they have done for my family. They truly showed, by example what the Body of Christ looks like. They invested their time into our lives, a priceless gift. My knowledge of what our responsibilities are as believers deepened because of this experience.

I have learned from this experience that it is not a choice but our responsibility to help if another brother or sister is in need. It doesn't necessarily have to be helping financially—it could simply be your physical presence or listening ear. If there is somebody in need who is in your life, don't turn your back on them. Don't stop answering their phone calls because it may feel uncomfortable. Jesus never turned anyone away regardless of what was on His plate. It is no coincidence who your neighbors are, who your friends are, who your co-workers are, who you go to school with, who you go to church with, and so on. God has strategically placed everyone in your life for a reason.

It was Spring Break 2005. Lauren had suggested bringing our boys to Branson for the week. Our boys grew to love these road trips to Branson,

Missouri we had been taking for a few years. Lauren truly allowed God to use her to minister to our family. In fact, Thomas recently had a school assignment in which he had to write about many "favorites." One of his favorite memories he listed were the many trips to Silver Dollar City in Branson with our friends. There was so much meaning behind this favorite. During some of Thomas' darkest days, trips to Branson stood out as a blessing and a sweet memory for him. Was that God using Lauren or what to bring a smile to my boys? God really does give us glimpses of Himself during storms. It's a lesson for me to be still and know that He is there.

God has strategically placed everyone in your life for a reason.

Despite our Spring Break week being a little rainy and cold, it was nice to escape a few responsibilities back home. I needed the relief. I needed to get recharged. Our boys seemed to have a blast despite the rain. Togetherness with their friends was everything. While we were in Branson, we had a lot of downtime, which was nice. Lauren helped me put together a menu for my first meal-making party. Initially, I was a little nervous, wondering if I could pull this off. There is plenty of pre-planning to have everything ready to prepare over 100 meals in one day! Normally, this would seem like an impossible task. That's because it was an impossible task! Lauren, being my faithful cheerleader, kept reassuring me I could do it. I'm glad she had confidence in me. However, the jury was out for me. Only time would tell if I would be able to pull it off. I kept thinking to myself, God you better be on my side for this one.

While we were in Branson, I figured it would be a great time to leave my eleven-year-old Volvo with Jessie, a member of our small group who works as a mechanic. He could take his time trying to figure out what was wrong with it. However, as we were driving back to Tulsa, Jessie called me with some rather grim news. He said he couldn't fix my car. The job was too big for him. I didn't panic but my heart sank a whole bunch. What in the world was I going to do now? As we were driving away from Jessie's, I remember Lauren grabbed my hand and said sister, let's pray! She prayed for a miracle! Her prayer was short and to the point as though the miracle would take place soon. Well, keep reading and find out about this big miracle! It's pretty amazing and unbelievable what God did for me. Later, Lauren admitted that, while we were praying, she sensed God was up to something big. I would like to pause here and point out yet another Fingerprint from God.

The Bible tells us that God will never leave us alone. In the Book of Psalms, He promises that He will be a husband to the widows and a Father to the orphans. These promises are repeated many times throughout scripture. This was a time I really needed a husband to lean on, with my car giving me so much trouble. God used Lauren to be my husband. She held me up with support, encouragement, and prayer like a husband is supposed to in his role.

Please continue to pause for a minute and let me paint a picture for you, God will use "His body" (other believers) to come alongside us in times of need. In our small minds, we may think we know what that looks like but often, we simply miss the moments because we are not still. If God prods someone in your life to reach out to you, just know that is God Himself connecting with you. Hence, this is why obedience is so important. We could miss out on God using us to bless somebody in need. And for us, the real blessing comes in giving rather than receiving. Though in my case, God had me in a humble season of receiving.

If God prods someone in your life to reach out to you, just know that is God himself connecting with you.

As Spring sprung forward, it was time to have my first meal-making party. Could I pull this gig off? Initially, I just wanted to get it over with. Both Lauren and Ann were such dear friends. They helped me pull off the impossible. I had fourteen people attend my first-round parties. Typically, most people have two parties in one day, morning and evening, which is easier when it comes to planning and buying perishables. I had sent out only one invitation to a few friends. God did the rest and brought them in! We were able to successfully prepare 112 meals in one day! Did you just notice this gigantic Fingerprint? Over the following months, I hosted an average of eighteen-to-twenty participants. We were preparing 160 meals in one day! You should have seen my shopping cart at Sam's Club the day before these parties. I had my flatbed cart overflowing! You can only imagine the stares I received by the time I made it to the checkout line. When the cashier would question me, I would smile and say, Oh I'm just having a few friends over!

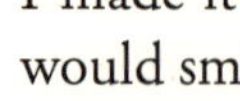

I was blown away at how word-of-mouth had gotten out about my parties. Remember, I hated anything remotely close to sales. This is what happens when you trust God with the impossible. What knocked my socks off, even more, was that I was making enough in one day to cover my monthly mortgage. I have no other explanation but God! He did it: He was my marketing coordinator! And the coolest part is that I was having fun at these parties. It was as though God was restoring parts of my old life. He was turning ashes into beauty. God was granting me opportunities to show hospitality again and I loved it! I was so very grateful for His gifts of grace.

Now I have a very special friend to tell you about at this point in my story. Her name is Beth. Getting to know her will change my life forever. As I mentioned earlier in this chapter, God was going to use that Sunday lunch at Ed and Sarah's home to change my life forever. Well, God pulled Beth into the equation. He was weaving Beth and Sarah into my life for a purpose: His purpose. God was connecting the dots and showing His Fingerprints all over the map. If you honestly think God cannot play matchmaker, then continue reading. He'll prove you wrong! And, the way He goes about playing matchmaker and setting the stage is pretty amazing, to say the least! With my story, all I can say is, Only God!

Beth started attending my parties from the very beginning, somewhat by accident. Of course, we know it was not an accident; and who was behind all of this? God! Beth had been a faithful customer of Sarah's and was unable to attend Sarah's next party because of scheduling conflicts. Therefore, Sarah referred Beth to my April party. I only knew Beth from church. However, her husband, Jordan, was one of the guys who use to be in Jeff's men's group, Iron Man. Here again, God was using this same group to minister to me years later. And here again, I'm getting to know another wife from this group. To look back, I thought God brought Iron Man into Jeff's life. Now, I can see His purpose. He brought them in his life a few years earlier for me. God knew all along what was going to happen down the road. He knew our marriage was going to end. He knew I would need a ton of support to see me through the darkest and hardest years of my life.

Amazingly, Beth and I connected instantly and became good friends. By this time, you should know this was not by coincidence. I just love how God can use His body, other believers, anytime. It's as though we had been friends for a lifetime. I remember when I walked Beth to the door at the end of my second party; she told me she was going to start praying for God to bring me a wonderful husband. I somewhat laughed and said, Sure, thanks. I was still in that season where I did not want to date anyone until God brought me my husband. I didn't want to waste my time. I didn't want to be a roadblock for God. I knew my choices stunk or at least my choices were not suitable for my best interest. Every time I bumped into Beth at church between parties, she told me she was praying. I always smiled and was very grateful for this new friend that God had placed in my life.

I didn't want to be a roadblock for God.

CHAPTER 19

The Contest of All Time

"To give them beauty for ashes"
— Isaiah 61:3a

Since Jeff had left our family, I had been struggling with the debt he left our family to bear. In addition, I still owed money to my attorney. Though, I will say I am so very thankful I did not incur one single dime of debt during the three years after he left us. Hello, was that not a miracle or what? On paper, it did not make any sense. Only by God's grace did He provide for me, as I know debt does not honor God. At one point, I had been approved for a loan, to refinance my home and get some extra cash upfront to pay Jeff's debt. The fact that I got qualified was a miracle alone, considering the state of my finances. I thought this was a good plan to pay off Jeff's old debt. Of course, God had better plans and blocked the loan from being issued. For whatever reason, Jeff refused to sign papers as his name was still on the house. I was in the middle of an appeal to get complete ownership of my home.

In the divorce, the judge had given Jeff 30 percent of the equity in our home, which was significant. In the divorce trial, he admitted he had spent all of our hard-earned savings on drugs and everything related to drugs. Plus, he left us with debt! I was left with hardly anything to survive. Justice had not been served in this Tulsa county court room. Immediately after the trial was over, I remember Kathy hugging me, encouraging me not to worry. She reminded me that God is our highest Judge; He will return *everything*. She then went on to say, Look at Job, he got everything back and then some! Nearly four years later, I still remember those encouraging words! Early on, I began to appeal to God for His perfect justice. I felt as though I had been wronged in court. I gave it all over to Him. My attorney suggested I file an appeal, which would ask the courts to give me full ownership of my home. Hence, if I won the appeal, Jeff would no longer be a co-owner of my home. My attorney advised that this appeal would probably take between six to twelve months to be heard. Here we go again, more waiting. Therefore, everything was on hold for the time being.

I had been hanging onto a mutual fund my Dad had given me after I had gotten married. It was down to $10,000. I was hanging onto it in case of a "rainy day." Ha! How about the last three years!? I never touched it. It was also hard to let go because, in a neat way, Daddy's gift was still helping me. I hadn't cashed it, but it was a safety net I had tucked away in the back of my mind. This gave me great comfort.

After I had gotten home from Louisiana in January, God spoke to me about cashing it in. He wanted me to pay off all of the credit card debt Jeff had left our family with plus paying off my attorney. Initially, I didn't listen to God. How in the world could I cash in my last bit of savings? I was hanging onto it for that rainy day! It didn't seem fair to pay off something that was not my fault. I didn't even incur the debt myself. And, it didn't seem fair to use this money, which was a special gift from my Dad for something ugly.

As the months passed, the conviction to cash in my mutual fund grew stronger. I didn't want to think about it: I blocked it from my mind. My good friend told me it was not honoring God by not paying off my account with a Christian brother, my attorney when I had money in the bank. Proverbs 3:27-28 states, *Do not withhold good from those who deserve it, when it is in your power to act. Do not say to your neighbor, come back later; I'll give it tomorrow when you now have it with you.* Don't you kind of hate when your friends are right? I know it had to take a lot out of her to speak truth in love to me many times. If she backed it up with scripture, she had my attention! Honestly, I don't think anyone really likes for someone to speak truth in love. Do you listen to them or think about what it costs them to be so bold with you? That's a true friend.

When May came around the corner, I could not honestly stand the convictions from God regarding my mutual fund. I could not escape God's still, small voice inside of me. I knew what the right thing to do was but I remained hard-headed for five months. Then it hit me...

Candy, you do not own your money, God does. You are trying to be in control, God doesn't like that. Candy, you are blocking God's blessings to your family when you try to control your life. Candy, you are telling God that you don't trust Him to provide for your family—and on and on. Ok, God had finally won! He always does. I had determined in my heart that I would do the right thing. God just had to deal with me for a few months. Oh, if we would truly trust Him from the very beginning, just think of the grief He would save us from! Ok, here's where you will see my hard-headedness shine through. I sat on my decision for about two weeks before acting on it.

I remember my decision came on a Wednesday, the last week of school in May. Late that afternoon, I remembered sitting on top of the kitchen counter with the phone in my hand. I took a deep breath and called the mutual company to cash in my fund. When I hung up the phone, there was a feeling of relief. It was done, I did it! Do you think God wasted any time with me once I followed through with obedience? Are you kidding? No way!

The very next morning, I received a phone call from the local Christian radio station, KXOJ. I had entered a contest a few weeks earlier and didn't give much thought about it. However, my letter was received after the contest was over. The radio station wanted to know if I still needed a car. I wasn't exactly sure where they were going with that line of questioning regarding my car. Before they hung up, they wanted to know when was a good time to reach me at home. Yeah, my suspicions were aroused to say the least!

Later that afternoon I was floored as I was driving home from running errands. I heard the afternoon DJ run a spot on KXOJ: Folks, just as we were packing up our boxes from the Contest of All Time, we received this letter that stopped us in our tracks. Join us next week as we will announce the winner live in person on the air in Broken Arrow! First, I screamed while I was alone in my car at a red light and then thought, No, it couldn't be. Were they talking about me? I'm quite sure the guy in the next car thought I was crazy!

Then the next day, I heard that same spot throughout the day. Yeah, anticipation was growing in me! The first thing that popped into my mind was that mutual fund I had just cashed in to pay debt. Was this in any way, shape or form a reward for obedience? I didn't have a clue but I felt as though God was up to something. Again, this is a feeling I couldn't explain. You just feel it.

Surely if God is up to something and wanting to bless you; then look out, here come the daggers from the enemy. Yes and unfortunately, the enemy is that predictable. His schemes have never changed, only the approach. My case was no different. Lauren always described certain individuals as hot fudge sundaes. One hot fudge sundae came back into town after being out of state for five months in a training program. He wanted to begin dating again. Up until his arrival, I had done very well. I had determined in my heart I would not date again until God delivered my husband on my doorstep standing on a silver platter! You may laugh but that was my desire. Besides, He told me He would do it during a quiet time in December 2004. I wrote about it a few chapters earlier described in Genesis 24.

I felt that if I went back on my commitment to God, then perhaps the unknown blessings that were about to unfold would be removed or blocked? I didn't know but I do know every time we step out on our own and walk away from God, there are consequences. Maybe not immediately, but eventually, the consequences will catch up with us. It may take us a while to connect the dots. Can you imagine how many times we have blocked blessings from God because we try to take control of our own lives?

Can you imagine how many times we have blocked blessings from God because we try to take control of our own lives?

It was nice to see my friend again. He had been away for nearly five months and wanted to begin dating again. I enjoyed his company. He made me laugh a lot. Though, this time around, I had the courage to be bold in my walk. I told him friendship was all that I was available for in this season of my life. He questioned me over and over on my reasoning. He didn't understand. I finally told him the truth. I said because I loved God more! I could not believe those words came out of my mouth. Then it felt really good to be myself and honest. Remember, I was waiting on God to drop off Mr. Right on my doorstep! I knew my choices and His choices were completely different. The first time around, I picked my mate without consulting with God and it ended in disaster. This time around, God could pick. I was determined not to get in His way!

The next day was Sunday and I was praising God for giving me a huge victory the night before. It actually felt so good to look in the mirror if that makes any sense? I took the boys to church and then we came home where we spent the afternoon together. That afternoon Thomas and Drew got out the hose and played in the water sprinklers. Most of our neighbors were outside enjoying the beautiful warm weather. However, things were a bit "cold" on my block. Some backs were turned and I wasn't sure why? Friendships had shifted some due to misunderstandings. Some friendships had shifted due to unexplainable reasons. Regardless, I wasn't sure why. The situation reminded me of verses in 1 Corinthians which Paul talks about yeast. It only takes a little bit of yeast to make a whole batch of bread rise.

The enemy loves to weave in dirt if possible to ruin something that was meant for good. I have learned through this trial as well as other circumstances that God knows everything: the good, the bad, and the ugly. And, I'm so thankful He is in control! I have also learned to bring your petitions to His feet when things seem so unfair. He is just and loves justice. He above all knows the entire truth. It's not shaded nor changed because of misinterpretations. I've also recognized He is the highest court. In other words, we can always appeal to Him when things are not fair here. He will vindicate you if warranted.

Late that Sunday evening after the boys had gone to bed, I brought my petitions to His feet. I decided to walk the property line outside my home. I began to pray asking God for His healing touch. I thought I was ready for change. I thought it was perhaps time to move out of my neighborhood and have a fresh beginning. Maybe it was time to move out of state to a new location? All I knew was that I wanted to be in God's Will where it was safe. That particular night, I fell to my knees in my backyard and asked God for help. I found myself so weary and tired. I wanted rest. Things, circumstances and situations were beginning to wear on me from the boys' father not being involved in their lives, our financial situation to grave miscommunications in my neighborhood. I had had enough. I know my Father heard my prayers. He tells us in Matthew 11:28, *Come to me, all you who are weary and burdened, and I will give your rest.* We are His sheep. Sheep are not weight bearing animals. Hence, we need to give our heavy load to our Father. After praying in my backyard, I walked back inside my house and slept very peacefully that night.

It was now Monday—thankfully, a new week. So much had happened over the weekend. Ann and I began working around nine in the morning as usual. Then about an hour later, life began to change. My Father was coming to my rescue with a big "Valentine." The doorbell rang, and it was the DJ, Dave Weston, from KXOJ radio station and David Miller from Trinity Restoration. Dave put a red microphone in front of me (almost in my mouth!) and said Hello with a big grin. He wanted to know if they could come in and give me some prizes. I had never in my life won a contest; I was a bit speechless. Thomas and Drew came running downstairs to see what the excitement was all about. They told me I was getting a car makeover! David Miller drove up to my home in a rental car and told me I would have the rental to drive while he restored my car. Then, David Weston gave the boys and me three tickets to Freedom Live—an annual event that KXOJ host every year in Tulsa.

Freedom Live typically has nearly a dozen Christian musical artists perform, and this particular year, the event was held at the Fair Grounds in Tulsa. Fans could move around between an amusement park and a water park while listening to concerts all day long. Was that cool or what?

That year, Freedom Live's performing artists were Michael W. Smith, Mercy Me, Hawk Nelson, Matthew West, Anthony Evans, Natalie Grant, and Sonic Flood to name a few. I was excited to get tickets for all three of us for this event.

Next, Dave Weston handed me a weekend getaway pass to any State Park resort in Oklahoma. To see the look on Thomas and Drew's faces when these prizes were handed out was priceless. It melted my heart. All during this time, Dave was recording my reactions. Anytime I would make an exclamation or comment, Dave would put that red microphone next to my mouth. He wore a big grin the whole time. He was obviously having fun with this giveaway. Then, we went out to my garage to look at my car. David Miller wanted a check-list of all of the things that were wrong with my car, and to clean it out because he was taking it back to his shop for a makeover! This next month was going to be so much fun for our family. Remember Lauren's prayer after we got home from Branson? God was answering her miracle-prayer in a much bigger way than either of us could have imagined. Isn't that just like Him? Another Fingerprint! In the midst of this opioid storm my ex-husband had gotten us into, God was showing His unfailing love to my family.

The next morning I heard the first radio spot while I was taking a shower. I laughed so much. I kept telling God how funny He was. He had this planned all along! KXOJ aired the first part of their visit with me when I first opened the door and heard Congratulations, you've won a car makeover! That segment played over and over that day on the radio station. The boys and I were pleasantly surprised every time we heard ourselves on the radio. Wouldn't you?

That afternoon, I received an email from Katherine Henson. She worked at KXOJ and wanted to congratulate me on winning the contest. She also began forwarding emails with the KXOJ commercial spots of our family on the radio. She said she would keep in touch with me over the next month and we would connect on the day of Freedom Live. During this next month, Katherine would be my contact person and she'd also became a special friend.

Every week leading up to the Freedom Live concert, the promos on the radio would change. New commercials were promoting the concert and new spots with the boys and me. It was so cool to be driving down the road and the next minute, I would hear Thomas and Drew's voices on the radio. We would just look at each other and laugh. I kept praising God the entire month thanking Him for the sweet experience. An experience I'm sure Thomas and Drew would never forget, myself included! It felt like Christmas—but it was different.

The way KXOJ promoted the concert and the commercial spots of my car makeover caused listeners to get excited and look forward to the big event. It was a real countdown. Towards the end of the month, I would hear spots like, Join us at Freedom Live when we unveil Candy's car live on stage in front of thousands. *Gulp*! There may be one big thing I haven't shared about myself in this book: I don't like talking in front of people. I have stage fright. It hit me, Candy, you are going to have to walk up on stage and not trip over anything in front of thousands and then put your thoughts together and say something intelligent. I started getting sweaty palms just thinking how I could get those keys without making a fool of myself on stage. So, I called Katherine at KXOJ very calmly asking her what would be required of me. I asked her if I had to give a speech or something and I shared with her that I did not like speaking in front of people—much less standing on stage in front of thousands. She understood and checked with her station manager.

Within an hour, she called back to reassure me that the only thing I would have to say was my thanks of appreciation. OK, I thought, I can handle that… I think? Then, I started thinking, OK, what if I tripped over wires or my two left feet? How could I quickly regain my composure? Can you see where my thoughts were going? That was the enemy trying to steal my joy… a tricky part of a huge blessing. So, I did the only thing I knew how to do: Pray. I'm like, Lord, you got me into this wonderful situation; you planned all of this. You know my weaknesses and fears. You made me and created me. You know what I am feeling right now; so, you handle it, OK?

I can only imagine God smiling but my fears were very real. And, God knew me. I think I started praying about my fears two weeks before the concert. Each morning, I would wake up and say Good Morning Lord, you've got fourteen days to calm my fears before I have to walk up on stage. Good Morning Lord, you've got ten days—and so on. You get the picture. Every morning during prayer time became a countdown. I remember the morning when it was three days until the concert. I woke up and told Him how many days were left… as if He didn't already know. Then, He gave me an answer that shocked me. He said, Oh, I am going to give you a taste of what it's like to be before many! I'm like, Lord, I don't want to talk about that, just get me through Saturday. I'm not sure exactly what He meant by that, but I wasn't ready to discuss it. All I needed was His grace to get through this event.

I will admit the boys and I were so excited about the day of Freedom Live. The boys were pumped about being able to hang out at Big Splash—a local waterpark—and Bells amusement park for the day. Unfortunately, not many of our friends or family were able to attend the event. I do remember what Lauren's older son said and it still touches me to this day. He said, "Mom, we have to go, we are the only family Ms. Candy, Thomas, and Drew have." We have to be there for them. Little did he know how deeply I appreciated his thoughtfulness? It was such a blessing to have friends there with us to share this experience.

Freedom Live was a long day, which lasted nearly twelve hours. We got there when the gates opened and immediately staked out our surroundings. Seating was not reserved, but rather, it was open-seating or standing-room-only. Then, as we got settled in for the day, I began scanning the fairgrounds looking for my car. I could not wait to see it, having heard so much about it on the commercial spots!

Then, we finally found it under a big canopy tent. Every door including the hood had been taken off. It was on display so everyone could get a good look at my car's makeover. I will say it was the shiniest I had ever seen it. As Thomas, Drew, and I walked up, our mouths dropped. There were new leather seats, which caught my attention first. Then, David Miller spotted us with a big grin and said, Well, do you like it? I was speechless because it looked like a brand new car. Most parts had been replaced. Everything was so shiny and new looking under the hood. I'm really not sure who was more proud of it, David or us. And when the boys saw the video monitor, you would have thought it was Christmas morning! You could see in their eyes they were putting two and two together. They could then watch movies and play their video games from the backseat.

As we inspected our makeover, I met Brian. He was responsible for reupholstering my seats. He said that after he heard the first radio spot on KXOJ about my car makeover, God told him he needed to be involved. He called David Miller offering his services. It was a great match since David's shop didn't handle reupholstering. Another Fingerprint! To top things off, there was another guy involved. His name was Joe.

More Fingerprints came along, with Joe involved in the makeover. Joe was responsible for installing my stereo system. He had just started his own business and it was located next to Brian's upholstering business. Brian had mentioned the opportunity to get involved with my makeover and jumped in feet first. This was no coincidence that their businesses were located next to each other. Remember, I had mentioned earlier that nothing happens by coincidence in this life.

About the time Joe got involved in my makeover, he had just taken a leap of faith in starting his own stereo installation business. As this was unfolding for Joe, God tremendously blessed him with financial backing from an owner of a major car dealership in Tulsa. Joe was experiencing his own personal "ride" from God! Isn't it so cool how God connects us together to share in these experiences?

It's hard to describe how that day felt for me—I truly felt like God's princess. It felt like He had rolled out the red carpet. Throughout the day, concerts were going on while fans moved between the two parks. Between concerts, announcements were being made that always pointed to *The Unveiling of Candy's Car* at the end of the evening.

That day, the boys had a blast, moving between Bell's amusement park and Big Splash. I owed a huge thank-you to Lauren's husband, Brad, who graciously took all four of our boys for the afternoon. Meanwhile, it gave Lauren and me "girl time." We stopped in a few times at David's tent, to visit with the guys who were responsible for my car makeover and I got the opportunity to know them better. They were awesome men of God who deeply loved the Lord. You could see the passion on their faces.

I remember one particular conversation I had with Brian. It was as though he was sharing prophecies about my future. Actually, it was God speaking through Brian. Remember how I shared in earlier chapters, God will use people in our lives to do and say things to us.

Brian said that winning this incredible contest was just the beginning for me this year. He said God was getting ready to do some BIG things in my life and that this contest was nothing. Well, *hello*, I was speechless. At first, he could tell that I was being polite about his comments but then he leaned in closer to get his point across. He said, Sister, God has some *big* plans for you this year; you need to just receive! *Gulp*.

During the day, I finally had the opportunity to meet Katherine Henson from KXOJ. It was like meeting a long, lost friend. She brought Lauren and me into the VIP building where all of the concert artists and workers ate dinner. She was such a sweetie. She wanted to touch base with me so we could be in contact with each other throughout the day. We were to meet back up at the tent before we went on stage later in the evening. Our presentation was scheduled between the last two concerts.

After that meeting, Lauren and I moved onto Big Splash to sit and unwind in the wave pool. We were able to "veg" and enjoy the afternoon. It was so surreal. Again, I felt like God's little princess that day!

Here's another sweet Fingerprint from God. Remember Kristie from the early days? (We went out to her family's lake house that first New Year's eve.) Well, her dad owned a business on the property between the parks. His office was on the second floor over the restaurant on the property. It was like a little apartment with a shower! Can any of my girlfriends read between the lines? A shower! Lauren and I had the opportunity to shower and get ready before the bigger concert that evening when my car would be presented to me. Again, God had the day covered for me. He took care of the little details that were important to me, like hair and makeup.

At this time, Lauren and I met up with Brad and the boys. Brad still looked like he was in good shape after spending the day with the boys. He was such a sweet blessing to me that day.

We were told to meet at the tent at 8 p.m. during the Mercy Me concert, which was the last show before Michael W. Smith came out on stage. Lauren and Brad took their boys to their seats while Thomas, Drew, and I waited at the tent for our time. By this time, the crowd had grown larger. It was estimated that there were approximately 25,000 fans there. There was a sea of people, and in the back of my mind, I started thinking that I was going to have to walk on stage and all of these eyes would be on me. I started feeling this knot well up in my stomach. But in the blink of an eye, that feeling disappeared. And, do you want to know what was ironic about that? Mercy Me was performing "In the Blink of an Eye" at that very moment on stage. That was God's humor as well as His perfect reassurance. Yet another perfectly-timed Fingerprint!

The evening was beautiful and my favorite part of the day was beginning… *sunset*! The sky was so beautiful and I felt God's presence. It was now time to take our "walk" through the crowd literally through thousands of fans as we made our way to the backstage area. The weather was beautiful with a slight breeze on that June evening. As were weaving through the crowd, Mercy Me was still performing "In the Blink of an Eye," Brian leaned over and whispered to me. Actually, he had to shout in my ear so I could hear over the music. He said, Sister, you are walking through the wheat fields and being sifted. The fans were symbolic of the wheat fields. And, now your Father is getting ready to deliver a crown. My car makeover was symbolic of the crown. He said, Don't forget, this is just the beginning for you! This was truly an incredible moment!

The next thing that happened was stinking fun stuff! It was like icing on the cake from God. We got to hang out backstage for at least an hour with all of these artists. It was so cool! We were standing behind the stage, looking out into the audience of thousands of people. As my fears would start to creep up, God would squash them immediately. At one moment, Dave Weston, the DJ from KXOJ, leaned over to Drew and Thomas to ask them if they were having fun. Dave asked the boys if they realized that every single fan in the audience would probably give anything to stand in their shoes. Thomas and Drew had the best seat in the house… backstage!

I could not believe that I was only a few feet away from Mercy Me while they were performing. I had walked up a few stage steps to get a better picture of the band and the security guy motioned me up. I could not believe that I was getting the opportunity to sit on stage inches away from Mercy Me while they performed. Was that sweet or what?

I will never forget the moment when they started singing "I Can Only Imagine." It was probably one of the most surreal moments I have experienced from God in my life. By this time, it was almost dusk. God had painted another beautiful sunset just for me! There was a slight, perfect breeze. I looked up and saw all of the scaffolding from the stage. I looked to my left and saw the drummer next to me. And I looked ahead and saw 25,000 people with that beautiful sunset behind them as Mercy Me sang "I Can Only Imagine." It couldn't have gotten any better if I would have planned it myself. For a moment, I felt my Dad smiling.

The song talks about how we can only imagine what it will be like when we get to Heaven. Wow, what a God-moment that was for me! I couldn't help but become overwhelmed with all of the sweet blessings God had bestowed on our family through this event. Not only was the car makeover a wonderful gift but also the excitement of experiencing the entire process left me speechless. God, Himself truly knows exactly how to lavish us with good gifts.

While Mercy Me performed, Michael W. Smith had arrived with his band and family. I was awestruck for the first few minutes. I had been listening to Michael W. Smith's music for at least twenty years! He is a legend in the Christian entertainment world. Unlike many worldly entertainers, Michael is very humble and genuine. It's hard to wrap your mind around the musical talent God has gifted him with.

While backstage, I felt like a little groupie, being around these great artists. When Michael walked by me, I'm not sure what came over me but I stepped right in front of him and asked for a picture. OK, honestly, maybe I *jumped* out in front of him. I can only imagine what must have gone through his mind. Being the gentleman he is, he smiled, giving me a big hug as we posed for a picture. He wanted to know if I was having fun at the concert. Again, everything was so surreal for me during those neat moments backstage. God gave me many little opportunities to chat with these artists. I had conversations with the lead singers from both Sonic Flood and Mercy Me. What struck me backstage was how gracious and *real* these guys were. I loved every moment!

Then, the time finally arrived. Mercy Me had finished performing on stage. The boys and I were the "act" between Mercy Me and Michael W. Smith. The boys and I were standing on the steps along with David Miller from Trinity Restoration, Brian who upholstered my seats and Joe who installed my stereo system waiting for our big moment. They were getting ready to give me the keys to my car in front of thousands of fans.

As we waited there, each of us had time to reflect on the previous month. It was as though they were an extension of my family. And, Biblically speaking, they are my family. It was neat how friendships had grown out of this experience. Joe had mentioned how he was getting a little nervous. And then, David started cracking jokes about the maze of electrical cords on the stage telling us to not trip over our two left feet. OK, his jokes were not helping any of us. As I started fighting the inner fears in my head about stage fright, I reminded God that it was His job to relieve me of these fears. He got me into this wonderful situation. Now He had to fix it and remove my fears.

Do you want to know what happened next? Well, as they called our names and it was time to walk up on stage, I was overwhelmed with peace. It was as though I was able to remove myself from my nervous body, sit back and watch the show. While I was stepping over electrical wires and cords, I was telling myself that this is a piece of cake. I was having a little conversation in my head with God. I kept telling Him that I couldn't believe how calm I was and that I wasn't nervous. I could almost hear God chuckle and say, I told you I would take care of all of the little details like Nerves! When are you going to quit doubting me, child? Another thing that I thought was comical; the stage lights were so bright that I could not see the audience. We were blinded by the glare and could see only a few rows of people rather than rows of thousands. Thank you, Lord!

The final touch of the evening was watching Michael W. Smith perform. I had the opportunity again to sit on stage while he performed. Again, this was too cool! An evening I will never forget.

CHAPTER 20

After the Contest

"With man this is impossible, but with God all things are possible."

— Matthew 19:26b

Freedom Live was one of the most incredible God-experiences I have ever experienced in my spiritual walk. Not only did He give me a much needed car makeover; He rolled out the red carpet and made me feel like a Queen for a day. It was one of those highs that really lasted. Not like when you are a kid and it's Christmas: All of the presents have been opened and played with; all of the Christmas dinner dishes have been put away until next year. As a kid, you lay in bed feeling rather blue thinking you have to wait another 365 days until next Christmas. You think that, in the next few days, the Christmas tree and lights will come down until next year. It's never exciting to put away Christmas decorations. It's not the same rush you experience when you are taking down the decorations. You can't wait to open up boxes and begin recognizing familiar decorations from the previous year. This is how Freedom Live's experience felt for me. It felt like Christmas but it was the wrong time of year. However, when all was said and done, the promotion spots on the radio ended and the concerts were over, I was still experiencing the high from the event, unlike the temporary highs you experience in other events or holidays. Another Fingerprint! I was still satisfied in Him. He wired us in such a way that there is only one true place we can be satisfied in this life. It's being content in Him, Jesus Christ.

God created us for one reason. He wants to delight in His children, *us*! Every single person on earth has a void in his or her heart that can only be filled by God. No amount of wealth, fame, prestige, or anything can truly satisfy and sustain us except God. And guess what, one important fact I failed to insert earlier? Remember the day before I got the initial phone call from KXOJ about my car needs? I had just cashed in my $10,000 mutual fund that my Dad had given me years earlier. Remember, I had trouble letting go, but I did it. Guess what my car makeover was worth? Would you have even guessed $10,000? That's exactly what God did; He returned it back to me dollar for dollar in a car makeover! A $10,000 car makeover! Can you say Major Miracle? The rest of the summer was the best summer the boys and I had in a long time. Somehow, God allowed us to take lots of little mini-vacations following Freedom Live. What I enjoyed most was watching the boys. I began to notice they were smiling a bit more often. I began to notice their smiles lasted longer. We were able to make trips to the lake, Branson, squeeze in a visit to Louisiana to see family, visit America's number one water park in the country and take our getaway trip from KXOJ's contest. I am really surprised how God allowed us to squeeze all of these trips in before school started again for Thomas and Drew.

He wired us in such a way that there is only one true place we can be satisfied in this life. It's being content in Him, Jesus Christ.

While we were traveling down to Beaver's Bend in Southeastern Oklahoma to enjoy our prized getaway, I remember I began telling the boys we had so much to be thankful for this summer. I tried to show them God's Fingerprints were all over us that summer. We were driving a car He fixed for us and He threw in some major perks like a DVD player to watch movies or play video games. How good is that? I explained that God delights in giving them the desires of their heart (Psalms 34). I wanted Thomas and Drew to see that even though we had faced some painful years that God pays attention to little details. He knows your heart. Only God can know your every thought. Nothing gets past Him.

It was July—seven months since God specifically spoke to me in Genesis 24. I say this so you can connect the dots at the conclusion of this book.

Towards the end of July, my friend, Beth, contacted me to see if I would be interested in meeting a friend of a friend. She claimed that she heard he was a *nice* guy. She didn't have much time to find out any details because she was leaving to go on our church's medical team mission trip down to Guatemala. OK, you get the picture, a friend of a friend! I told her sure, you can pass on my contact information. Well, I immediately began to pray asking God to keep this guy OUT of my life if he was not supposed to be there. I did not want to become friends with a guy if God didn't want him to be there. I had already been down that road a few times; I didn't like the results when I made my own decisions. It was almost as though my prayers were negative rather than positive.

I had finally reached a point for the first time in my life that I was completely satisfied in God and no one else. It wasn't fun getting to this point, but in hindsight, I'm thankful for the way that it happened. This is where God wants us to begin with—vulnerable and open to Him—but for some reason, many of us are always searching for more. Though, our journey will never be complete until we reach Heaven.

I do need to insert another important event here that will help you connect more dots on this journey. For about six months, God had laid it on my heart to stop at a friend's house to pray. Marla lived in the adjoining neighborhood. Every time I passed her house, God kept telling me that I needed to stop in to say hello and pray. Marla and I had known each other from Moms in Touch and from church. She had helped in Kids Zone at church for many years. Plus, we had been in a ladies Bible Study together. I loved Marla who is such a sweet spirit.

It seemed as though every time I passed her house, I was always in a rush and never had time to stop. One day, I could not ignore God's convictions any longer, so I stopped in to say hello. It was nice to catch up with her. She and her daughter had just gotten back from our church's last medical mission trip to Guatemala. In fact, Beth was on that same mission trip.

During my visit, Marla had a heavy heart and shared some personal things going on in her life. She needed a prayer warrior to stand in the gap with her. I agreed to stand with her and lift up her needs in prayer. We prayed and as I was getting ready to leave, she stopped me and asked if I was dating anyone. I told her no. She then asked if I was OK with that or was it time to meet a husband. I had to laugh; I love her sense of humor. I told her I was content not dating, but that if God had somebody in mind, then bring him on. She then told me she would stand in the gap and pray for a Godly husband. Wow, little did I know why God wanted me to stop by Marla's. Can you begin to connect some dots? Many of my friends seem to be on the same page. What if I would have been disobedient and not stopped at her home; just think of the blessings I would have been robbed of? Nearly a month had passed by since Beth called about mystery guy. I was continuing to have my monthly meal making parties. God was continuing to use these parties as a blessing to me, which covered my mortgage. I was amazed at how faithful He was in providing for our family during this season in our lives. Each month, we never came up short. During my August meal-making party, Lauren was pumping Beth for information about this mystery guy. By this time, Beth had more details. Lauren had concluded that this guy was exactly what we were looking for. Excuse me, "we." Since he had never called me, I assumed that was God's protection over me because I had specifically prayed asking God to keep him away from me if he wasn't supposed to be in my life. The thought of meeting mystery guy was out of my mind but not Beth's. When Beth got home from my meal-making party, she contacted her friend to find out what was taking this mystery guy so long to call me.

Apparently, Beth's friend never checked her email with my contact information. Her friend immediately called the mystery guy and told him he needed to call me because I was a very nice person. By this time, the mystery guy was not interested in meeting anyone. His life had become very busy with his new business, and he thought he didn't have time for anyone new in his life. I think as a courtesy and because Beth's friend was persistent, this guy finally called me to be done with it.

When the mystery guy finally called, we talked for nearly two hours on the phone. He seemed like a nice guy. We had a few things in common but nothing special hit me. After we hung up, I had to look on caller id to see that his name was Ralph. I think at the beginning of the phone call, he introduced himself and I was very nonchalant about the whole situation. Honestly after we hung up, I didn't think I would hear from him again. It was no big deal to me. Perhaps that is exactly where God wanted me.

As the summer was winding down and school was beginning, our church was planning another mission trip. Each year, our church takes approximately four mission trips to a church we help sponsor in

Guatemala City. This particular trip was their annual children's mission trip. In years past, our church had introduced the "Backyard Bible" programs during the children's trips. After one trip a few years ago, Thomas voiced a desire to go on a mission trip to Guatemala. I told him, One day. Well, this time around, Thomas began asking me again if we could go. I thought in the back of my mind that there was no possible way we could even imagine going on a trip like that because we were still surviving on meager means. Then, I heard His small, quiet voice in my heart say, "So Candy, you don't think I can do it for you?" I'm like, OK Lord, you're right, as always! I thought to myself, Gee, He sure showed off with Freedom Live. So, I told the boys we would pray about this trip. Thomas, Drew, and I held hands in our living room. I told the boys we should lay our petitions before God because that's exactly what He instructs us to do. Come boldly to His throne. So, I began to pray on behalf of our family. I prayed, Lord, we want to serve you in Guatemala. You know better than we do which mountains you need to move for us to go. So, we give this trip to you. We will accept your will.

The boys were very excited thinking about the possibility of going on a mission trip to Guatemala. I reminded them it might not be His will for us to go down there for whatever reason. It's as though they already knew in their hearts the answer. God brought to mind what Brian had shared with me earlier in the summer. He said Freedom Live was just the beginning. Our summer was full of little adventures. Was a mission trip to Guatemala God's next gift to us? I didn't know; all I knew was that it was in God's hands because a trip like that was definitely not in my budget. I didn't exactly like the idea of asking for money. A friend had commented that God uses His body in so many ways. There are seasons in life of both giving and receiving. Giving is much easier than receiving. It doesn't necessarily involve humility. Though, humility grows a necessary building trait of character. However, giving may require some sacrifices while being obedient to God. Regardless of which end God has you on, some blessings follow both giving and receiving. We sent out one support letter to a few and left the rest up to God.

CHAPTER 21

A Sunset to Always Remember

"He performs wonders that cannot be fathomed, miracles that cannot be counted"

— Job 5:9

It was now Labor Day weekend, our last "hoorah" of the summer. Boys were now twelve and eight years old. They were growing up so fast and had already experienced so much life in a short time. Whenever my heart would begin to break for them about our situation from the wake of this opioid addiction, God would always remind me of the verses in Daniel 3 that all three of us would come out of this trial without the smell of smoke.

Even though the landscape of our neighborhood had changed some, boys were still grounded with friends. The Turner family had become very special to us. As always, God crossed our paths at the perfect time. They had lived in our neighborhood all of these years but became a special part of our family two years earlier following Jeff's walking out on us. My neighbor, Ann, had been long-time family friends with them and was instrumental in connecting our paths.

Mick and Gwen had initially invited us to their home to participate in a nationwide study that was taking place in many churches and homes across the country. It was called the Purpose Driven Life. Many of you may be familiar with the study. That initial study with them was the beginning of what would become a long, sweet friendship. We would begin to do life deeply with them. They are one of those families where we would swap kids back and forth sleeping over at each other's homes. They were a source of spiritual support that was priceless during a season in our lives when we needed that kind of support the most. Again, God using His body in the way He intended it to be used. Another Fingerprint! I will always be forever grateful for Mick and Gwen's friendship. There is something supernatural about their home. Not only do you sense God's presence when you walk in the door but there is always an overwhelming blanket of peace there. Even when driving by their home, I sense a supernatural peace if that makes sense.

Getting back to Labor Day weekend, it was now Saturday evening. The days were beginning to get shorter—those long summer nights were coming to an end. This particular day, Thomas, Drew, and Colson Turner had been playing together all day. It was one of those marathon weekends where playing never ceased. They went back and forth between each other's houses. As the day was coming to a close, I could hear the boys playing in the field behind our house. So, I went out to my backyard to read. It was a beautiful afternoon and I so enjoyed hearing the sounds of laughter coming from my boys.

As I was reading my Bible, God told me to get up and look at the sunset. At the time, I really didn't know what God was up to but nevertheless, I got up and looked at the sunset. Oh my gosh, it was the most beautiful sunset I had ever seen. My thoughts immediately raced back to that sunset I had seen in December from my childhood home in Louisiana. Remember a few chapters earlier, when I talked about the word God had given me in Genesis 24? As I began to look into this sunset, He began to point some things out to me. The sun was radiant shades of pink, red and orange. It was absolutely gorgeous. But more incredible were the white clouds that encircled the sun. It was as though God painted the clouds to taper and reflect a long bridal veil around the sun. God said, See, it's going to be much bigger than you can imagine!

Initially, I didn't understand what God was trying to show me. I kept questioning Him on what it could be. Then, all of a sudden it hit me—the sunset was a picture of my future husband and wedding. It was going to be more beautiful and bigger than I could imagine. He even whispered in my ear that he was coming into my life sooner than I could imagine! I remember questioning the Lord, Are you sure? OK, it seemed a little surreal but then again, look out when God gives you a word. He is faithful and He doesn't break promises. Not one place in the Bible is there a record of a broken promise from God. So, why would He start now?

After a few minutes of taking in this sunset, it was beginning to get dark and time to go in. I figured it was time to corral the boys in as well. When I walked into my kitchen, I had the nerve to question God about what I had just witnessed. I asked Him, Lord, are you sure about this? It was as though I could hear Him laughing. I then went into my garage to see what the boys were up to because I had heard them earlier on their bicycles.

The next thing I witnessed was God's humor and confirmation of His word. As I walked out on my driveway, I could see Drew and Colson riding their bikes towards me singing "Here Comes the Bride!" OK, I let out a scream and questioned them immediately on why they were singing THAT particular song! They gave the cutest explanation. They had been riding their bikes in the field behind our house and it had been a little muddy. So, their tires were muddy. Along my side-yard, I have a white picket fence with at least a dozen Althea or Rose of Sharon bushes planted. This time of the year, my shrubs were blooming hundreds of beautiful lilac flowers and my sidewalk was covered in blooms that had fallen off. As the boys were riding their muddy bicycle tires on the sidewalk, the fallen blooms were sticking to their tires like potpourri! Hence, "Here Comes the Bride!" I could not stop laughing and told God that He was very funny. OK, He definitely got my attention! I was floored and I knew He was up to something. I decided to enjoy the ride and allow God to have complete control. I had to get out of His way. Shoot, I couldn't plan anything this wild even if I tried. Again, just think what I would have missed out on had I chosen a path of self-will (disobedience).

The next thing I witnessed was totally God's humor and confirmation of His word. As I walked out on my driveway, I could see Drew and Colson riding their bikes towards me singing "Here Comes the Bride!"

God also brought to mind another sunset that I talked about in Chapter 12. It was my drive home with Ann down the Muskogee turnpike. We had just seen the conditions where the boys' dad was living. I had an incredible knot in my stomach, life seemed hopeless for the moment and God spoke to me in that beautiful sunset telling me that He was going to take care of us. Bottom line, He is always talking to us, are we listening?

It is so amazing how God has used sunsets in my life to describe so much to me. Perhaps He knows He has my undivided attention when I notice a beautiful sunset.

Later the next evening, Ralph called me for the second time. We were both free that Sunday evening and had a lot of extra time to talk on the phone since the next day was a holiday. Four hours to be exact! I am not sure exactly where the time went but we seemed to have a lot in common. Again, I didn't think much of his phone call, other than that he seemed like a nice guy who was turning into a friend. Geez, did God ever have me exactly where He wanted me! I was so content and satisfied in Him. I've often heard that's when God can do amazing things. Are you connecting any dots?

Over the next few weeks, Ralph's phone calls started to increase. We were becoming phone buddies discussing the problems of the world. I will admit I was becoming a bit curious of what he looked like. I knew his voice. Even more curious was my best friend, Lauren. I hesitate to insert one of the funniest stories here, but it is just too good to pass up.

One day Lauren was shopping at a local furniture store that also had a restaurant inside of it. She knew that Ralph's business partner owned the restaurant and he spent most mornings there eating breakfast. Ever heard the old saying, curiosity killed the cat? Well, that was Miss Lauren! She was on a spy mission for the both of us! There was a good chance Ralph could be there. While Lauren was sitting down eating, she noticed a black man dressed up at the counter giving the waitress a hard time telling her that she worked for him. This man fit Ralph's description to a tee including the baldness! However, there was one little exception, this man was black. During some of my conversations with Ralph, he mentioned that he had gotten very tan over the summer hanging out at the lake.

Well, like most girlfriends, Lauren immediately called me with the news. However, I detected something in her voice. I questioned her on whether he was ugly or something. She hesitated for a while and said he was definitely dark but not from the lake rather dark from the gene pool! It was apparent that Ralph was a black man. Please let me insert a disclaimer here. I am not against interracial marriages but it was not something for me. She then asked what I was going to do. Well, there was only one thing I could do. I called Beth immediately! She wasn't home but you can imagine the long, drawn-out message I left on her answering machine. I'm sure she had to laugh when she heard it.

Later that evening, Ralph began instant messaging me on my computer. We chatted for a while sending messages back and forth to each other. Then, Beth called me back with answers. I told Ralph to hang on for a while because I had an important phone call to take. Little did he know what that phone call was about! Beth had contacted her mutual friend who said Ralph was not black. She thought Ralph was of Swedish descent. However, I have to share here that Ralph is not of Swedish descent. He is far from it—he has a mix of Hispanic and Irish, which is a far cry from Swedish. By now, this situation had become a storyline right out of a *Seinfeld* episode! We laughed about it for a long time. Still, to this day we laugh about it!

But bottom line at this point, nobody had seen what Ralph looked like. It almost became a mission to find out what the mystery guy looked like. I wasn't exactly interested in dating him yet but *geez*, curiosity had gotten the best of me!

CHAPTER 22

Answered Prayers

"There is a time for everything, and a season for every activity under the heavens."

— Ecclesiastes 3:1

Two weeks had passed by since I had sent out our only support letter in the hopes of going to Guatemala. Every day, the boys would come home from school asking if we had received anything in the mail. When I would tell them nothing had come in, I could see the disappointment on their faces. I would then try to convey to them that this was all about God. If nothing came in, then God definitely had other plans for us.

Meanwhile, the drama of seeing what Ralph looked like was mounting. He finally asked me if I wanted to meet for coffee. However, long story short, he canceled our coffee because he got cold feet. Of course, he didn't share that when he canceled our coffee date; he claimed he was very busy and didn't have time to invest in a relationship. The truth is that he was afraid that he was beginning to like me, which was not on his schedule that he had mapped out in his mind. Because his business was beginning to take off and he was involved in some Bible courses at his church, he wanted to focus on that first and not allow any distractions. Ralph was trying to share that he didn't want to look for a wife until his business had grown some and he had finished this yearlong course at his church.

I accepted his reasons but we were on opposite sides. I was only interested in friendship at this time. Immediately, Beth called me wanting to know what Ralph's excuses were. She felt bad because she was involved in setting us up. She was a little miffed with Ralph because he bailed before our first meeting. So, she called their mutual friend to make sure Ralph's story to me added up. During this season, I had a lot of overprotective friends, which I appreciated!

Beth did call me back and verified that Ralph appeared to be on the up and up and was completely honest with me. He told his friend the same reason for canceling our meeting. He basically didn't want things to move forward on a deeper level. Was Ralph putting God in a box? Don't you love that God's time table is almost always different from ours?

Ralph's tough stance didn't last too long. He called me later that evening and talked for about three hours, and he ended our call by inviting me to his church the next morning.

The time had finally arrived to meet the mystery guy! Thankfully, our church had a big lunch planned after service so I was able to get away after dropping off the boys at church to meet Ralph at his church. In a neat way, I thought it was very fitting to meet him for the first time in church. Was this all part of God's plan? Did He foil our first meeting in a coffee shop to orchestrate a better setting, church? Initially, I didn't know but looking back, YES!

My anticipation grew even stronger waiting for Ralph to show up at his church. The service had already begun and he was fashionably late. I hesitated walking into the service knowing I could miss him completely. The time finally arrived when I saw Ralph walking toward me. I recognized him because he told me he was bald, which was all I had to go on. He was nicc-looking but didn't seem to be my type, though I really liked his smile. I considered him a good friend or a good buddy. After church, we chatted for a while but I had to quickly leave because I needed to head back to my church to pick up my boys.

Imagine the anticipation from my friends? They were dying to know what the mystery man looked like. For some reason, Lauren was pleased that we didn't have any initial chemistry between us. She said that was good because being attracted to each other would be a distraction and it would not give us a chance to develop a genuine friendship. OK, sure, whatever, I thought. I didn't exactly follow her line of reasoning but I allowed her to continue being my surrogate overprotective mother. Nevertheless, I loved her honestly and deeply valued her wisdom. The next week was the final week to turn in registration and money for the children's mission trip to

Guatemala. In my heart, I just assumed it would not be this trip. I trusted God and truly believed that He didn't provide because it was not in His will that our family go to Guatemala. The boys seemed very disappointed.

Lauren was pleased that we didn't really have any initial chemistry between us. She said that was good because being attracted to each other would be a distraction and it would not give us a chance to develop a genuine friendship.

During that week, I was able to reconnect with Brother Henry, the pastor who had come over that same day Jeff left our family. He was the one who had cupped his hands around my face wanting to know what I wanted. If you can remember earlier chapters, I told Brother Henry I wanted to be able to stay home with Drew until he started first grade the following Fall. Nearly three years had passed since that painful day. There was a lot of catching up to do. I had shared what had been going on in my life and was able to share that God answered all my prayers about staying home. I was happy to share that I was still able to stay home thanks to the small medical billing business that my neighbor and I had started. Another huge Fingerprint!

Brother Henry being who he is, he inquired if I had started dating. I did share about my friendship with Ralph. Immediately, his antenna went up and he told me to bring Ralph by his office so he could give him his approval or not. Again, I was so grateful to be surrounded by protective friends who genuinely cared about our family. I also told him about the mission trip and how this trip was not going to happen for our family. The deadline was in three days and we had not received a dime. It seemed pretty impossible to come up with nearly $3,000 in that short period of time. Though, it was truly fine with me because I knew deep down in my heart that God had other plans for us. I hated the part about the boys being disappointed but thought it would be a great teachable lesson for them.

After visiting with Brother Henry, I came home to finish some work before the boys got home from school. What happened in the next few hours will forever be remembered in my heart. It was one of those moments you always remember. For instance, many of us remember where we were when we heard that the Challenger Space Shuttle blew up or what we were doing when we started hearing reports about 9/11.

After I got home, I walked out to my mailbox to pick up my mail and saw a letter from Dan and Celeste, former next-door neighbors who now live in Texas. It appeared to be a check and I immediately thought to myself that I was going to have to send it back. It would not come close to being enough since we were running out of time. When I opened the letter, I was speechless! The check was enough to cover all expenses for the boys. Dan attached a sweet one-sentence note, I think this would be a good experience for the boys. Oh my gosh, I'm sure the neighbors could have heard me screaming throughout my house.

I immediately called Dan and Celeste to thank them profusely. Instead, I got their answering machine. So, I left a long, drawn-out message to them, thanking them over and over. Later, Celeste called back and said her son wanted to know why Miss Candy was so excited. I'm sure he could hear the excitement in my voice. I then called Ann, my neighbor, to share the good news. She was equally shocked. What a huge testimony of God's grace and power. His timing may not be early but it's never late either. Wow! Ann mentioned that she would be happy to keep Drew if needed. I told her thanks but I already knew in my heart that God was going to come through for us.

During the next two weeks, God came through in a mighty way. He provided enough to cover all three of our expenses including the extra expenses to expedite our passports, spending money and extra money to donate back to the trip! *Hello*, have you ever heard of such a thing? As my friend would say, He was showing off! I cannot begin to share how much this impacted Thomas and Drew. They were ecstatic, to say the least! How good is God? He allowed my boys to travel on this mission trip with their best friends who they had been traveling with to Branson over the last two years. Another big adventure for them! Remember what Brian told me at Freedom Live? The best was yet to come! His words were coming true.

Ralph continued to call me and his frequency of calling tended to pick up to almost daily. We were truly becoming good friends. A solid foundation was developing. He was excited to see how God was working in our lives regarding our mission trip. He was preparing to leave for a four-week job with his business, right about the same time we were supposed to leave for Guatemala. It was almost a coincidence that we were departing at the same time to travel to opposite ends of the country.

Ralph had started coming over for dinner and hanging out with me. One particular night, he came over after working a church function. I was in the middle of watching a movie. It was *My Big Fat Greek Wedding*. We laughed a bunch watching this movie. After it was over, he leaned over and kissed me—something I was not expecting from a friend. But what was weird (in a good way) is that it didn't feel at all like I was kissing my brother. It triggered some feelings that I didn't expect were there. Hello, was this God slowly playing Cupid? Regardless of what God was doing, I was rather speechless.

Hmmm, what was going on? Oh, don't you just love it when God's hand is in it, the absolute unexpected happens! To my recollection, nothing ever happens the way I imagine it when I allow God to take the lead, it's always better! Do you see a theme here? What happens when you give up and submit to God? What happens when you genuinely trust Him? Incredible things happen like my car makeover, like our mission trip to Guatemala, and the shifting of my relationship with Ralph into a new direction. Is God not amazing?

Well, immediately our relationship changed and I loved that we had become friends first. A lot of things were beginning to happen. We both had a week before we left on our trips. As Ralph was preparing to leave on his business trip, we were getting ready for our mission trip. At church, we were packing all of our supplies for Upward Basketball. We deflated nearly 100 basketballs, packed nets, jerseys, cones, etc. Each mission team member brought an extra empty suitcase to pack our supplies. It was an exciting time. I was looking forward to getting to know other members on our mission team that I didn't know well.

Meanwhile, Lauren was assisting God in this cupid expedition. Would it be any other way? She thought it would be nice if we double dated with her husband. This way, Lauren could finally meet mystery man in person and both she and her husband could "interview and screen" Ralph to see if there were any red flags. I agreed and thought it would be a great idea.

Our double-date ended up happening the night before we left for Guatemala. Ralph seemed to have an instant connection with Brad and Lauren. I almost felt like a little girl waiting for Mommy and Daddy's approval. I trusted their judgment and couldn't wait to hear their thoughts.

Now the test of time was getting ready to happen. Will it be either of the old sayings, Absence makes the heart grow fonder, or Out of sight, out of mind? I gave our relationship to God. This is the first time I think I almost prayed against a relationship that I was interested in. I truly did not want Ralph in my future if God didn't want him there. And, I asked God to reveal this to me while we were apart from each other for the next four weeks. Ah, it would be the test of time.

CHAPTER 23

Mission Trip Guatemala

"The harvest is plentiful but the workers are few."
— Matthew 9:37

The time had finally arrived for our mission trip. Six weeks prior, we were clueless that our family would be traveling together on a mission trip to Guatemala. You just never know when God has something up His sleeve. Marla—my neighbor and friend who I prayed with two months ago—had called me the day before telling me that she wanted to bring us to the airport. Thomas and Drew were so excited about this trip. When we got to the airport, we saw all of our team members checking in. Marla stayed for a few minutes with the other families who were saying their goodbyes. We all held hands in a circle and prayed for protection over our trip. It was a neat experience. I already felt such a strong bond with my team. We were all there for one purpose: to serve Him.

While we are at our gate, Ralph began texting me a lot. I mean like every minute. I think it had just hit him that we would not be seeing each other for four weeks. Louise, our mission coordinator, asked if I was getting text messages from my husband. She was clueless about my situation. Lauren just grinned and said no, she is getting messages from her boyfriend. Louise said OH in rather a curious way. Lauren continued to grin and told Louise that "we" like him.

We had twenty-three people on our team. The next week, we were getting ready to share life deeply and get to know each other much better. We had twelve kids on the trip. Since this was fall break, all the kids were missing two or three days of school. Many of them brought schoolwork with them to work on while on the plane. We had only one stop from Tulsa to Guatemala and that was Dallas. As soon as our plane landed in Dallas, my cell phone started buzzing with text messages. I got a few stares and a few grins. Lauren said I bet I know who that is! Yep, it was Ralph, continuing to text me. He was so funny.

We had enough time on our layover to grab a bite of dinner before our flight to Guatemala. On the next flight, we were split up more since we were on a larger plane. So, we paired kids up with adults. Lauren took Caleb and Drew who sat in the front and I took Thomas and Jake and we sat in the back of the plane. Thomas and Jake played with their Gameboys while I sat back and listened to music. I had recently purchased Casting Crowns new CD and was looking forward to listening to it. Nearly every song spoke to me and I will never forget one surreal God-moment. Remember in earlier chapters how I mentioned that sometimes God speaks to me in songs. One particular song, "Praise You in the Storm" just hit me.

And what made the moment so surreal while I listening to this song very loudly, I turned to my right looking out of the window and I saw the sun setting in the clouds. I turned to my left and I saw the moon while the clouds next to the plane were racing by. Then I looked down next to me and saw Thomas and Jake just laughing so hard at *something*. With them, one can only imagine! I felt overwhelmed by God's presence. This trip was a gift from Him. I was still in the storm but I was praising Him. He lifted me up so many times when I was down. To this day, every time I hear this song on the radio, I'm reminded of this particular moment.

Shortly after I heard this song, our plane began to experience some moderate turbulence. Before our head-on collision, turbulence on planes never bothered me. However, after our wreck, any turbulence would put me on edge. When the turbulence began, I started to pray, OK Lord, you gave us this trip and I know you don't lead us down the road of calamity, please calm my nerves. Almost immediately, He gave me a vision. It was Jesus holding our plane in the palm of his hand. He told me not to worry one bit on this trip; He had it covered. Then I had this sweet peace for the entire trip.

We arrived in Guatemala City late Saturday night. Lenny, our church's missionary, and a member from Shalom church met us at the airport with a bus to take us to the seminary where we would be staying for the week. Kids were tired, excited, hungry, and all the rest. I didn't realize just how big Guatemala City was. It's about 2.5 million in population. You could immediately smell diesel fumes of the city—a smell we would get used to over the next week. On the way to the seminary, we pulled over at a McDonalds to get some food. Most of our team was famished and ready to eat anything. Kids were excited to see a McDonalds in another country.

When we finally arrived at the seminary, I was amazed at how beautiful our surroundings were. The seminary sat on a few acres surrounded by brick walls and guards at the gate. The campus was amazing. There were dorms rooms on one end, a basketball court and a playground in the middle with offices and meeting rooms on the other end. The seminary was an oasis in the middle of Guatemala City and our kids had lots of open space to run. This would become our home away from home for the next seven days.

Our first morning in Guatemala was Sunday. The bus came to pick up our group and bring us to Shalom Church. I was looking forward to church. One reason is because I have heard of Shalom Church for so many years while attending Liberty Church back home. It was our sister church that we supported. Many of us have heard Pastor Lopez preach at Liberty, our home church. I have seen many slideshows from previous mission trips. Many in our group had connections with Shalom Church members.

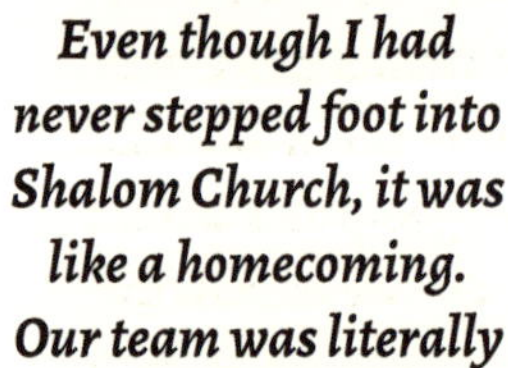

Even though I had never stepped foot into Shalom Church, it was like a homecoming. Our team was literally greeted with open arms.

Even though I had never stepped foot into Shalom Church, it was like a homecoming. Our team was literally greeted with open arms. Pastor Lopez had our team to line up in front of the church while the church members came through and greeted us. It was like a processional line at a wedding. In one sense, these strangers were hugging each one of us like long lost family members. But then again, isn't this the way God created His body? Jesus is the Bridegroom and "The Church" is His Bride. When He comes back, it will be our "Homecoming." These members were so grateful for our desire to serve them. Life in Guatemala is much more difficult for them compared to our comfortable lives back home, yet there is such a sweet simplicity in the way they do life. They get it! They get the basics of life, whereas we get weighted down with all of the stuff in our lives that we miss the important things that matter most. Or at least this was what God was speaking to me that Sunday morning.

After church, we came back to the seminary for a wonderful home-cooked American meal. Louise had arranged for the kitchen staff to cook American meals while we were there. This was a big *plus* for our kids! Later that afternoon, we regrouped and got ready for our week of basketball camps. We inflated 100 basketballs that we brought with us, got nets and supplies ready for the week. Then, Jimmy and Dwayne got the rest of us ready, with basketball drills that we had been working on for a few weeks.

Later that same Sunday afternoon, Lenny took Jimmy and Dwayne to scout out the basketball courts we would be using that week for Upward Basketball camps. We had a pretty good idea that the courts would be in poor condition. We knew we would have to take brooms to sweep off dirt from the courts and bring our own nets for the goals.

The courts at each location appeared to be in fair condition. However, they were concerned with one major problem. The courts that we would be using in the afternoon camps did not have rims on the goals. Without rims, we could not put up basketball nets. Without nets, there would not be any shots that could be made. Without scoring shots, there could not be any games played. This could have been a deal-breaker. However, this was not a deal-breaker for God. Jimmy and Dwayne figured we could improvise—somehow, someway.

Guess what? The next afternoon when we arrived for our first-afternoon camp, there were metal rims on those goals! Remember: We were in Guatemala, a poverty-stricken country. Basketball was not a popular sport there. Having these rims to be fastened to these goalposts would have required a welder with welding equipment. *Hello*, did we experience a miracle or what from God? Another Fingerprint! We all looked at each other and smiled because we knew without a shadow of doubt that this was a miracle. It was one of those moments where we shook our heads, laughed and said, Thank you, Lord! Let's play basketball!

Our Upward Basketball camps consisted of two sessions a day. In the mornings, we went to one neighborhood in the city, and in the afternoons, we went to another neighborhood on the outskirts of Guatemala City. Signs were put up the week before announcing our free camps. Attendance was great and even higher than we imagined. Each day, our sessions grew in numbers. Each day, we recognized some of the same sweet faces. They showed up everyday wanting more. Sadly, many wore the same clothes every day. At the end of each session, we would share the gospel and two of the kids from our team would share their testimony.

Hearing Thomas and Drew share their testimony via a Spanish interpreter was worth the entire trip for me. It was priceless, especially knowing the current trial going on in our personal lives. Their dad had walked out on them but God did not. A few friendships had turned cold, but God did not walk away. He had sustained us in the midst of this valley. I am always in awe of His faithfulness. Providing our family with the opportunity to go on this mission trip is a perfect example of His faithfulness. It was a wonderful week that I will never forget. Not only were the lives of Guatemalan kids touched forever but it changed our lives, too. God gave me glimpses of what He called us to do.

Before He left this earth, He told His disciples to feed His sheep. The harvest is plenty but the workers are few. I now have a very small glimpse of how big that harvest really is. New friendships and memories were made to last a lifetime.

The times I have come home from being abroad always reminds me just how blessed we are as a nation. I am grateful Thomas and Drew had this incredible experience that they could never learn about in a textbook or a classroom.

The boys were happy to get home. Waiting for us at the airport was Marla, my sweet neighbor and faithful prayer warrior. She was an unexpected pleasant surprise since I hadn't made any arrangements on how we were going to get home from the airport. Well, God took care of that for me because He knew I had forgotten about those little details. Marla wanted to hear all about our trip. She had just gone on the previous medical mission trip to Guatemala so the culture and everything about Guatemala was still fresh in her mind. We both agreed that it was an experience of a lifetime. At this point, I would like to encourage anyone who has never had the experience or revelation of going on a mission trip: GO! It will change your life and awaken areas in your life that perhaps you never knew existed. Giving is so much more gratifying than receiving.

CHAPTER 24

Would You Be My Girlfriend?

"Those who hope in the Lord will renew their strength; they will soar on wings like eagles; they will run and not grow weary; they will walk and not be faint."

— Isaiah 40:31

Now back to reality. The mission trip was over and our lives continued just like before—only now with a much greater appreciation of blessings.

It had been a week since I logged onto my computer to check my emails. Actually, it had been nice to be detached from the Internet. However, I discovered nearly a dozen emails from Ralph. He was anxious to hear from me. It had now been a week since I had seen him. The distance was good in a way. It gave me a chance to think and pray about my friendship with him. I had missed his company but I still didn't want him in my life unless God approved of him. I trusted God. I didn't trust myself. I knew God wanted His best for me. My heart was in His hands. I wanted to play by His rules because I knew God would protect me regardless. I knew God was with me.

I trusted God. I didn't trust myself. I knew God wanted His best for me. My heart was in His hands.

Ralph was very happy to hear my voice and I was happy to hear from him. He was going to be another five weeks in Illinois with his company doing a final clean on a major distribution facility. He wanted to fly me up to Chicago the following weekend.

I laughed and told Ralph that would be next-to-impossible. I had been out of the country for a week and I had commitments as a mother like being home with them for a while. So instead, he booked a ticket to fly home the very next weekend.

His determination to get home ASAP to see me convinced me that his feelings toward me were genuine. In the very beginning, we had set some very specific boundaries in our relationship that honored our respect for each other and more importantly, respect for God. So with that in mind, his actions spoke volumes to me and continued to earn my respect.

So with that in mind, his actions spoke volumes to me and continued to earn my respect.

It had now been two weeks since we had seen each other. Perhaps a little absence does make the heart grow fonder. At least it was beginning to seem that way. Ralph and I spent most of the weekend together, catching up. From the very beginning of our friendship, we logged many hours talking to each other either in person or on the phone. It was not uncommon to talk three or four hours at a time on the phone; we never ran out of things to say. As the weeks went by, we realized that we had more and more in common than we realized.

It was so bizarre in my mind, because on the surface when I first met Ralph, I didn't think he was my type. But in reality, was "my" type right for me? It wasn't in the past! This time around, God was totally in control and He knew what He was doing! Ralph and I clicked from the get-go. Almost like a brother and sister relationship. And, what I truly appreciated most is that we became friends first with no agenda to date.

The weekend went by way too quickly. Before I knew it, I was driving Ralph to the airport to catch his flight back to Illinois. He said he would call me when he got settled back in his hotel room. Before I made it to bed that evening, Ralph was calling. He had made it safely back to Sterling, Illinois. Even though we had spent the whole weekend together, we must have talked on the phone that night for hours. I was getting tired and told Ralph that I needed to end our call and get some sleep. However, this particular phone call ended in a way I didn't expect. It will be one of those phone calls that I will always remember as it definitely caught me off guard. As we were getting ready to hang up, Ralph asked me if I would be his girlfriend! It was such an old-fashioned gesture, which I appreciated.

Through the decades, it has been called going steady, courting, going out, dating, etc, etc.

Ralph wanted to make our relationship exclusive, giving us a chance to discover whether or not we had a future together without the threat of dating others. In my mind, I immediately went back to previous conversations I'd had with God. The kind of conversations where I did all of the talking and God graciously allowed me my moment. I reminded Him of all of my prayers to remove Ralph from life if he wasn't supposed to be in it—as if God needed to be reminded! Inch by inch, God nudged us closer together. Ralph and I were so compatible. We never ran out of words to say. I'm in total awe of God's handiwork in our relationship. In the beginning, never would I have imagined us together in a romantic way. Jeez, don't you just love it when we get out of God's way. Stuff happens! In a good way! I think about how there must have been many times in my past and, of course, will happen in my future, when good gifts from Him are delayed because I'm standing in His way.

Ralph would be stuck in Illinois for another three weeks before his project would be completed and he could return home. We continued to talk on the phone daily for many hours and our relationship continued to grow. I was really looking forward to his return. I felt this incredible peace about our relationship. It was a kind of peace that I had never experienced before in previous relationships. Ah, the missing link: God. This time I was allowing Him to lead. In return, I got to experience His peace. Again, this was one of those supernatural feelings that I cannot describe in words. Trust me.

I think about how there must have been many times in my past and, of course, will happen in my future, when good gifts from Him are delayed because I'm standing in His way.

When Ralph finally came home, we picked up right where we left off. This time, it was different. We were in a committed relationship and exploring the possibility of a future. I *so* respected his old-fashioned approach towards our relationship.

Ralph returned on the weekend of Thomas' birthday. Ralph had briefly met the boys a few times earlier. They seemed to have a connection. This time, we invited Ralph out to dinner with us to celebrate Thomas' birthday. Dinner went well; Thomas and Drew seemed to enjoy Ralph's company. I appreciated the fact that Ralph never tried to push himself on the boys. He gradually began spending more time with them. During this time, I began to discover yet another side of Ralph. He was and is like a big kid. Ralph loves animated movies and video games. OK, that alone was almost enough to qualify Ralph as their new best friend! I watched the boys as they began to gravitate towards Ralph on their own. His attention towards them was genuine and they knew it.

As Ralph and I began taking intentional steps of getting to know each other better, we started the best habit together. We started praying together, on our knees. Before we ended every night together, Ralph and I would pray. Initially, it wasn't exactly comfortable but we knew it was a foundation that pleased God. It grew our relationship tremendously. When it's genuine and you're praying out loud with someone, you get glimpses of their heart. Statistics say that couples that pray together, stay together. I like those odds!

Before I knew it, Christmas was here. This particular Christmas was very special because Ralph was in my life. That Christmas spirit was in the air. I had so much to be thankful for in my life. Since Jeff had left us, the preceding few years had been rather difficult to celebrate Christmas. Sure, I decorated our home, but many of my actions were for Thomas and Drew's sake. Christmas is such a big deal for kids. I never wanted my grief or lack of Christmas spirit to be sensed by them. My heart had been so broken for them and what they were experiencing in their young lives as children of divorce. I wanted to shield them and protect them.

Our old fake Christmas tree was nearing the end of its life. It had seen better days. To say it looked like a Charlie Brown Christmas tree was an understatement. Likewise, Ralph hadn't celebrated Christmas in a few years since he was single. He went through tremendous pain with his family following his ex-wife leaving him. His world had crumbled, too, and God had brought in dear friends to provide support and help him pick up the pieces. This year was different for both of us. Restoration was beginning to take place. Ralph brought over his twelve-foot Christmas tree, which hadn't been used in a few years. He helped us decorate it while listening to Christmas music. Imagine how fun that was! Sweet traditions were being gently restored. It just felt right. Then again, only God!

We continued to have long conversations. Still, we never ran out of things to talk about. We continued down this path as God continued to intentionally nudge us together.

This Christmas we had made plans to go home to Louisiana. It was time to share with my family about Ralph. I was looking forward to spending this Christmas at home. The boys always loved going home to see their grandparents and cousins. This particular Christmas, we had made arrangements for Thomas and Drew to stay a week longer and hang out with their cousins. I was also looking forward to a break. As a single Mom, it's tough because you don't have a spouse to watch your back or give you much-needed breaks.

As much as I enjoyed spending Christmas in Louisiana, I was more excited about going back home to Oklahoma to see Ralph. We would have a few days without the boys to date. Things were a bit different when I returned. Ralph seemed very distracted. He was excited to see me but something was on his mind. He seemed to be elsewhere. He was almost nervous. I began to question him about what was going on.

I will never forget the look in his eyes as he told me that everything was just fine. For a minute or two, he fumbled his words and then the Big L word came out of his mouth. He told me that he was falling in love with me and wanted to spend the rest of his life with me. Whoa, wow, *hello*—I was speechless! Yes, literally speechless. I was silent for what seemed like a few minutes. Then, out of my mouth came the same words. Yep, it was one of those moments in my life I will never forget! And guess what time of the year it was? New Year's Eve! Remember many earlier chapters in this book I shared about how my friend, Lauren, was grieving that first New Year's Eve when Jeff left us. And God gave her a distinct word that I would be celebrating on New Year's Eve. She had imagined it would be the following year not three years later. Once again, God always keeps His word! It almost seemed like a fairytale, but God was writing new chapters in my life. Also, remember what Brian told me at Freedom Live? Initially, I smiled but he leaned closer to me to get my attention. He said that the best was yet to come. Freedom Live was just the beginning. Well, looking back at the year since my car makeover, God had knocked my socks off! Is this multiple Fingerprints or what?

It almost seemed like a fairytale, but God was writing new chapters in my life.

In a small way, this reminds me of the story with Abraham, when God told Abraham that he would have a son. Though, Abraham never dreamed he would have to wait twenty years until that Word was fulfilled. God told Lauren I would be celebrating on New Year's Eve. We just didn't dream it would be three years later. God spoke through Brian that the best was yet to come for me. He is always faithful and never late. I never dreamed the celebrating would be about my impending marriage! Incredible things happen when you allow Him to write your story.

Incredible things happen when you allow Him to write your story.

Ralph brought me over to his parent's home to meet them. They were having a party with long-time family friends. What a way to be introduced to his family and no doubt checked out! While looking into a sea of faces smiling at us, Ralph's mom makes her way to me to introduce herself. She is a very lovely lady and was everything he had talked about. Carmen made me feel very welcome in their home. I also had the opportunity to meet his dad and sister. They were all very kind.

CHAPTER 25

Setting a Date

"Now hope does not disappoint, because the love of God has been poured out in our hearts by the Holy Spirit who was given to us"

— Romans 5:5

It was a brand new year: 2006. I was falling more in love with my future husband. We were beginning to talk about when and where we would be married. However, we still had a few necessary steps to take as we moved forward.

It was finally time to meet Antonio, Ralph's stepson from his previous marriage. At the time, Antonio was only fourteen years old. By the time I finally met Antonio, I felt like I knew so much about him. Ralph had spent many hours talking and sharing about Antonio. Ralph was so proud of the young man Antonio was growing into. I was so looking forward to getting to know Antonio better. He was only one year older than Thomas. Our boys had a lot in common and we were looking forward to the boys getting to know each other better.

Next, Ralph wanted to ask Thomas and Drew for my hand. He didn't want the boys to think that he was here to sweep me away from them. By this time, they were beginning to know Ralph better. Ralph was slowly earning their trust. When Ralph told Thomas and Drew that he loved me and wanted to spend the rest of his life with us as a family, they grinned and liked the idea. I can only imagine what was going through their young minds. They had been through so much; stuff that kids should never have to experience in their lives. I did not want to see them this heartbroken again.

This is why it was so important for me to follow God. He had our best in mind. I did not want to step out in intentional disobedience again. I desperately wanted God's blessings on my family. Too much was at stake. When it comes to Thomas and Drew, I am like a mother lion, *don't* mess with my babies. I would never allow a relationship with another person to compromise my relationship with them. I am very protective over them, to say the least. Just think, if I'm this protective over my boys, how much more protective would God be? More than any of us can fathom!

While Ralph and I had been planning and talking about our future, Ralph had never officially popped the question. He kept telling me it was coming and would be a total surprise. Well, let's just say he shocked the you-know-what out of me! He told me it would be the unexpected and it was!

It was a Wednesday morning about 9:30. I would have never dreamed in a million years it would have been a weekday proposal! Ann and I had been working for a few minutes when I received a phone call. Caller I.D. indicated it was KXOJ—yep, the same radio station that I won my car makeover with the previous summer. I thought to myself, What in the world do they want with me? The DJ introduced himself and asked for me. Then he said, I have somebody that wants to talk to you. I'm like, OK! The next thing I know, Ralph is also on the phone!

Between the radio station and Ralph, they had made arrangements to do a three-way call. Ralph started to tell me how much he loved me and wanted to spend the rest of his life with me, all while on the air. The next thing the DJ told me to do is walk to my front door and answer it. Hmmm, did I have questions? You bet! When I looked through the peephole of my front door, I saw Ralph standing there holding something. It was as though I was moving in slow motion. The DJ then told me to open the door. Again, all of this was on the air!

Ralph was standing there holding a silver platter with a gift-wrapped box on it. There was a yellow sticky note attached to the gift. The note read, "Special delivery from God." By now, the DJ was wanting play-by-play for the listening audience. I was totally floored. He had my ring gift wrapped in a box on a silver platter! Oh my gosh, I was speechless. How cool was that?

Remember a year earlier; God had specifically spoken to me in Genesis 24. The passage is about Abraham sending his servant out loaded with treasures in pursuit of a wife for Isaac. Through these scriptures, God told me He would bring my husband on a silver platter. Once again, God kept His word. In my opinion, one word best describes my Father: Faithful! I might also add that between the time I received that word from God and the time I found out about Ralph was seven months. Keep the number 7 in mind for later chapters.

Ralph was grinning ear to ear. He said doing it on a Wednesday morning would take me off guard rather than the more traditional approach on a weekend night at a restaurant. Well, hello! He definitely surprised me!

KXOJ played our proposal on the radio for several days. It was fun. Many of our friends got to hear it on the radio along with the city of Tulsa! Ok, was God knocking my socks off or what? My point is, get out of His way! Who can write a love story like this? This is another huge Fingerprint on my journey. Let's call it a double, triple or even quadruple Fingerprint here! God just loves to show off!

Who can write a love story like this?

Our next big challenge was in deciding when and where to have the wedding. We had both been down this road before and had big weddings. We wanted to make it all about us rather than pleasing everyone. I don't mean to show any disrespect here but if you have gotten married before, you know exactly what I am talking about. The preparation can steal precious moments because you are caught up with all of the details of planning a wedding. We wanted a small wedding and didn't know where to draw the line on whom to include while being sensitive to important people in our lives.

Guess what we did? We planned an elopement! Talk about fun! However, we had trouble coming up with the right date. After it was all said and done, I think we moved our date up three times. You can do that kind of stuff when you're eloping! We were older. We knew what we wanted and we wanted to honor God with our relationship. Ralph was getting ready to leave town for Maine. His company had gotten a contract to do a job in Lewiston, Maine. We were thinking it would take between four-to-six weeks based on previous jobs. We both knew we didn't want to wait that long.

Ralph proposed to me on February 8th and we eloped two weeks later, on February 24, 2006, in Eureka Springs, Arkansas! Not sure exactly how we were able to pull off all of the details from finding a chapel, lodging, and someone to keep the boys for the weekend. Amazing how everything fell into place in so little time but it did! Only God! We have been blessed beyond with best friends in the world! Our day would not have happened if it were not for the help of our dear friends.

We found a beautiful chapel in the Ozark Mountains, overlooking Beaver Lake. Everything was perfect, like a fairytale. While I got dressed in my wedding gown, Ralph had some extra time to spend outside on the deck. This was the time that he used to be reflective and pray. He said he gave God permission to stop our wedding if it was not supposed to happen. He, too, desperately wanted God's blessing on us. Ralph said that as he finished praying, he looked up and saw a beautiful bald eagle soaring over the lake right in front of him. He said it was such a surreal moment for him and knew without a shadow of doubt that God was with us.

Our ceremony was quiet and elegant. We were in the mountains and our backdrop was the lake. How good is that? The actual ceremony was pretty traditional but we will never forget the words our minister spoke over us. Our minister spoke about how our marriage would involve service or ministry work together. We would be involved in helping others. It wasn't like a few comments but our minister spent a few minutes talking about how we would be serving others together. Continue reading on and see how these spoken words over us really come true.

After the ceremony, Ralph and I drove around the lake to our cabin to begin our Honeymoon. As we were driving up this steep and winding incline to our cabin, we saw five eagles circling above. Do you think God threw that in for extra good measure? It was such a sight to behold. These eagles were so beautiful and majestic. It almost felt like God was wrapping His arms around us and telling us how pleased He was with us. Again, He was showing off!

CHAPTER 26

A New Beginning

"Delight yourself in the Lord, and He shall give you the desires of your heart"

— Psalms 37:4

It was time to come home and begin a new life together. We were anxious to pick up the boys and bring them home. I know they must have had so many thoughts running through their minds of the unknown. Yet, I know at the same time, they were excited to be getting a new step-dad. We had only two weeks together before Ralph left for Maine. It's almost like God already had these details figured out. Well, actually, He did! This time gave the boys an adjustment period before Ralph left. It was like baby steps of getting them used to Ralph being around.

I do need to insert here another big Fingerprint. Remember in earlier chapters, about my appeal? In my divorce trial, the Judge had awarded Jeff a large portion of the equity in my home. It appeared that justice had not been served in the courtroom. Six months later, with the encouragement of my attorney, I filed an appeal to hopefully win full ownership of my home. Rick mentioned that an appeal could take as long as six to twelve months to be heard by a group of judges. Neither of us ever dreamed it would take twenty-one months!

Ralph and I had been married for a few days when I got an unexpected phone call from Rick, my attorney. He left this long message on my answering machine. He said that I had finally won my appeal! The judges had awarded my home to me, free and clear, with Jeff's name being removed from ownership! Again, one word to describe God: Faithful! I was reminded of what my friend, Kathy, had told me immediately after my trial when I thought justice had not been served. She said I could appeal to a higher court, God. He does get the final word. Nearly two-and-a-half years later following my trial, justice had been served!

Getting us back to the story, Ralph's project in Maine lasted much longer than we both anticipated. Seven weeks to be exact! That's a long time to be apart when you are newlyweds! However, we did have the opportunity to have a second honeymoon fairly quickly. My mother was kind enough to fly up for Easter to stay with Thomas and Drew, while I flew to Maine to spend some time with Ralph. It was so much fun being together in New England in the spring. We explored famous lighthouses up and down the coast while having opportunities to eat fresh lobster. I never realized just how charming and how much the state of Maine had to offer. Not only beauty but also rich in history.

Our week together in Maine went by too quickly. I hated leaving Ralph behind but it was time for me to come home. School was nearly over for the boys and there were lots of activities still on the calendar that needed my attention. Ralph came home three weeks later. Within days of his return home, his dad passed away from a lengthy illness. Even though it was a short time, I am thankful that the boys and I got to spend some time getting to know his dad.

Now that Ralph was home, it was time to settle in and begin our new life. The blending of our family was nothing short of supernatural. I had heard many stories from other people about how the most difficult part of a second marriage is the blending of families. This was not the norm with us. It was as though Ralph had been with us forever. Ralph immediately started backing me with the boys. He didn't force himself on the boys as their new stepfather, but rather, he was consistent. He was my backup that I didn't realize how much I had missed when I was a single mom. He had my back. And, Thomas and Drew respected Ralph being consistent with them. Whenever they tried to pull the wool over my eyes, he would call them on it. They could no longer get away with things that I had let slide for a long time. I never had a discipline problem with the boys. The fact is, they were in desperate need of male mentors in their lives. It had been over three years since they had a father figure in our home.

In those early days, Ralph was so good about doing family stuff together like playing games. He always included the boys in activities including chores! He began to play an active role in their sports, school, and church activities.

Moreover, I am grateful for the way Ralph's family welcomed Thomas and Drew with open arms into their family. They made Thomas and Drew feel special and accepted. They desperately needed to be loved by others. It was so beautiful how this transition took place. They truly went out of their way to welcome them into their family that first year. Not only did they welcome us into their family, but they also welcomed all of my close friends into their extended family!

It has now been seven years since I first began this book. It took me a while to get started but God never let up. Seven is a very significant number in the Bible. It represents completion. Seven days to complete the earth, among other things. When God gave me a Word in Genesis about my future husband, seven months later, I learned about him. Ralph and I knew each other for seven months before we got married. Five years ago, in my mind, I thought I was finished writing this book. God told me, No. Little did I know He would finish this book with a husband! So, it has now been seven years. Remember Brian at Freedom Live concert? The best is yet to come? He was not kidding about that prophetic word from God!

Remember our pastor who married us who said we would be involved in serving others together? Ralph and I have completed our third year together serving in our Youth department at church. Three years ago, God granted us the privilege to start working with high school freshman, which happens to be Thomas' class. We have moved up with this same class and will begin our final and fourth year with them in a few months before they graduate. Words cannot begin to describe the incredible blessings we have received as a result of this service. God has used us and stretched us beyond what we would have ever imagined. I have loved every moment! There is such a huge degree of satisfaction when you are in His will.

There is such a huge degree of satisfaction when you are in His will.

Seven years later, I am a different person. God has refined me more than I could have ever imagined. I see life with a different set of glasses. My priorities have been shifted to what is important. I'm not "there" yet but I'm closer. Even though I was a believer in Jesus Christ before this journey took place, my eyes were focused on different treasures. Worldly treasures had my attention. Prestige, accumulation, and affluence were used as a guide of measure. Unfortunately, these things were little gods in my life. It took my attention off the grand prize. If I hadn't lost nearly everything in my life, would God have truly gotten my undivided attention? I don't know. I do know that there are so many people that walk through life thinking they are happy and content with what they have until they lose it. What happens when your world is turned upside down, who or what will you turn to?

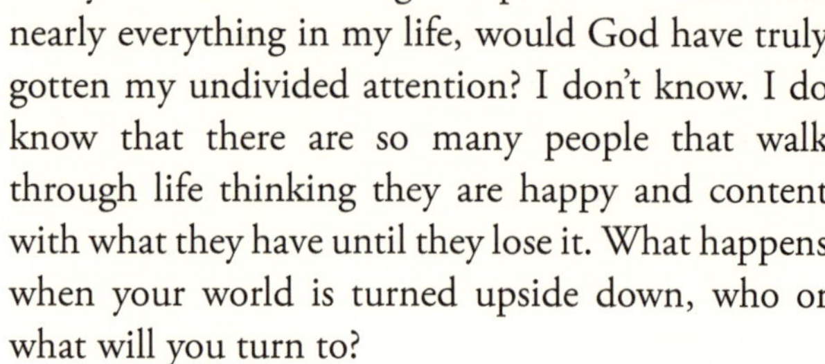

If I hadn't lost nearly everything in my life, would God have truly gotten my undivided attention?

Addictions are real. Addictions can come in the form of opioids, other drugs, alcoholism, pornography, etc. I have learned so much through this painful journey. When I measure events on my lifeline, I can say without a shadow doubt that going through a divorce and helplessly watching the death of my family due to an addiction far outweighs any other events on my lifeline including the death of my father to cancer. Through this experience, I've been graciously granted wisdom. How will I use this wisdom? First of all, I know that my boys' father's side of the family has struggled with addictions for several generations. It was something their dad was keenly aware of and did not want any part of it. But yet, his family's generational addictions got the best of him. While he thought he heeded their mistakes, he was not strong enough to overcome those strongholds/addictions.

We are all weak, but by God's grace, He blesses us with wisdom and strength. He gives us wisdom to run from addictive behaviors. For example, why would you want to take your first drink of alcohol if you come from a long line of alcoholics in your family? Why play Russian Roulette? I have learned that there truly is no such thing as coincidence. Coincidence is a mere disguise. I hope I have encouraged you to fight the good fight. I hope I have dispelled the myth of divorce. Unfortunately, I use to believe in that myth until it happened to me. Divorce can be like a cancer; it is a death of a marriage and often leads to the death of other relationships. You don't know how to treat it, especially when it happens to family, friends or even you. Please let me encourage you from first-hand experience, you can walk through it with God's help. We have lived in a fallen world since Adam and Eve. Nothing is perfect on this side of eternity but we are blessed with God's abundant grace. If you have family or friends experiencing divorce, walk with them through it. Don't avoid them or abandon your relationship with them. They are in so much pain; don't add to their pain. Stand in the gap with them. You may be pleasantly surprised at how God will use you. Don't run away from blessings. Remember, God is always honored when we step out of our comfort zone for Him.

CHAPTER 27

An Update on Life

"And the God of all grace, who called you to his eternal glory in Christ, after you have suffered a little while, will himself restore you and make you strong, firm and steadfast."

— 1 PETER 5:10

IT HAS NOW BEEN sixteen years since I first began this journey of recording the mountains that God moved on our behalf due to my ex-husband's opioid addiction. It was also the number of years (16) I was married to my ex-husband. So much has happened since those early days of my separation. Perhaps God will prod me to write "Part 2—After the fairytale wedding"?

I finally did reach a point after seven years that I was able to forgive my boys' father.

I would like to share some more good news through this process: I finally did reach a point after seven years that I was able to forgive my boys' father. The process of letting go was truly freeing for me.

I first recognized this moment of freedom during my older son's high school graduation party in our home. When it came time to send out invitations to Thomas' graduation party, I paused for a moment on whether to send Jeff an invitation to the party in our home. I followed my gut like I'd done in the past and asked myself what would be in Thomas and Drew's best interest? The answer was simple.

Jeff came to Thomas' graduation party in our home. He had the opportunity to reconnect with old neighbors and friends. Initially, these old neighbors and friends were apprehensive when they first saw Jeff in our home. Totally understandable. Though, I reminded them this party was about our family celebrating Thomas. Jeff did stay for most of the party and seem to enjoy connecting with old familiar faces. In fact, he was the last guest to leave the party.

After he left, it hit me that I had truly forgiven him. I know that if I had not, it would have gotten under my skin that he was in our home. Hence, I would have been robbed of the joy of celebrating my son's high school graduation. God is good to give me the grace to forgive. Holding onto anger, hurt, or sorrow does not benefit anyone. For one thing, it's not Biblical. It's not healthy either. Forgiveness brings such freedom. I chose life!

Sixteen years is a long time to reflect on lessons learned from this extremely painful time in my life. Would I ever want to go back and have a do-over? Absolutely not! Recovering from a life-threatening injury or grieving the death of a beloved family member hurts. However, recovering from betrayal is raw and brutal.

Sixteen years ago the world didn't know the meaning of an opioid addiction. I did. I screamed in silence for help. Nobody understood or could relate to me. Thankfully today that has all changed. We know so much more today than we did yesterday.

I think it's hard to sum up in a few paragraphs what I have learned through the process of an opioid addiction. First of all, if you believe a family member, friend, coworker, neighbor, or that you are struggling with an opioid addiction, tell somebody! There is help available. Don't walk this journey alone. I would not be standing today if it had not been for my strong network of friends who held me up when I was weak. God gave us community for a reason. We are not to travel through this life alone; He made us dependent on each other. Find a small group or support group. These are places where you can draw your strength. You are not alone. Look for Fingerprints from God.

I have walked through some of my darkest hours that were ignited by an opioid addiction. Today, I am living proof that there is beauty from ashes. I am thankful for a faithful Father who truly cares about all of the details in our lives. Thank you for allowing me to share my story. I choose hope. I choose life. I survived and you can, too.

What is Salvation?

I DIDN'T WANT TO CONCLUDE my story without sharing about how to invite God into your life. One particular relative who read my story was going through similar circumstances tried to tell me I was different. She said that the God she knows would not do the same in her life. That is quite the contrary. First of all, there is absolutely nothing special about me other than the fact that I love Jesus.

The only way to truly know Him is spending time with Him in His Word (the Bible). If you have to dust off your Bible, then perhaps there is a good chance you don't have an intimate relationship with Him? Religion is man-made. A relationship is God-made. Let me give you an example to offer a better understanding of a relationship with God. Do you have friends that you either see or talk on the phone with every day? Also, do you have friends that you might see every few years? Which friends do you know better and more intimately? Of course, your answer will be the friends who you spend time with regularly. The same applies to God. How will you truly know God if you are not spending time with Him? There is more to life.

How do you become a Christian?

This is the best part. Because of God's love for us, He made it exceedingly simple to become a Christian. First of all, you don't become a Christian by joining a church or adopting a creed. There are lots of false churches, false creeds, and even the devil believes in God. All you have to do is receive Jesus as your Savior, fully accepting His death as the sufficient sacrifice for your sins (John 3:16), fully trusting Him alone as your Savior. Again, becoming a Christian is not at all about rituals, going to church, or doing certain things while refraining from other things. Becoming a Christian is all about having a personal relationship with Jesus Christ. A personal relationship with Jesus Christ, through faith, is what makes a person a Christian.

Christianity outlines God's plan for the world. It is the story of creation, fall, redemption, and restoration. Creation refers to God as Creator. He made the universe and all that is in it. The first words of the Bible echo this reality: *In the beginning, God created the heavens and the earth.* (Genesis 1:1)

Originally, all that God made was good, including human beings. Our relationship with God functioned as He intended it to function—in harmony. But after what Christians term as the Fall (original sin), some things went very wrong, breaking our relationship with God and resulting in a threefold strife between God and us, between one another and within ourselves.

The Bible describes sin in many ways. Most simply, sin is our failure to measure up to God's holiness and His righteous standards. We sin by things we do, the choices we make, attitudes we show, and thoughts we entertain. We also sin when we fail to do the right things. The Bible affirms our own experience: "there is none righteous, not even one." No matter how good we try to be, none of us does the right things all the time.

To go into more detail, here are a few scriptures to give you a better understanding of what God did for us; thus, paving the way for Christianity. People tend to divide themselves into groups—good people and bad people. No matter how we might classify ourselves, this includes you and mc. We are *all* sinners.

> *"For all have sinned and come short of the glory of God."* — Romans 3:23

Many people are confused about the way to God. Some think they will be punished or rewarded according to how good they are. Some think they should make things right in their lives before they try to come to God. Others find it hard to understand how Jesus could love them when other people don't seem to. But I have great news for you! God DOES love you! More than you can ever imagine! And there's nothing you can do to make Him stop! Yes, our sins demand punishment—the punishment of death and separation from God. But, because of His great love, God sent His only Son Jesus to die for our sins.

"God demonstrates His own love for us in this: While we were still sinners, Christ died for us." — Romans 5:8

For you to come to God you have to get rid of your sin problem. But, in our own strength, not one of us can do this! You can't make yourself right with God by being a better person. Only God can rescue us from our sins. He is willing to do this not because of anything you can offer Him, but JUST BECAUSE HE LOVES YOU!

"He saved us, not because of righteous things we had done, but because of His mercy." — Titus 3:5

It's God's grace that allows you to come to Him—not your efforts to "clean up your life" or work your way to Heaven. You can't earn it. It's a free gift.

"For it is by grace you have been saved, through faith - and this not from yourselves, it is the gift of God - not by works, so that no one can boast." — Ephesians 2:8-9

For you to come to God, the penalty for your sin must be paid. God's gift to you is His son, Jesus, who paid the debt for you when He died on the Cross.

"For the wages of sin is death, but the gift of God is eternal life in Jesus Christ our Lord." — Romans 6:23

Jesus paid the price for your sin and mine by giving His life on a cross at a place called Calvary, just outside of the city walls of Jerusalem in ancient Israel. God brought Jesus back from the dead. He provided the way for you to have a personal relationship with Him through Jesus. When we realize how deeply our sin grieves the heart of God and how desperately we need a Savior, we are ready to receive God's offer of salvation. To admit we are sinners means turning away from our sin and selfishness and turning to follow Jesus. The Bible word for this is "repentance"—to change our thinking about how grievous sin is, so our thinking is in line with God's.

All that's left for you to do is to accept the gift that Jesus is holding out for you right now.

> *"If you confess with your mouth, "Jesus is Lord," and believe in your heart that God raised him from the dead, you will be saved. For it is with your heart that you believe and are justified, and it is with your mouth that you confess and are saved."* — Romans 10:9-10

God says that if you believe in His son, Jesus, you can live forever with Him in glory.

> *"For God so loved the world that He gave his one and only Son, that whoever believes in him shall not perish, but have eternal life."* — John 3:16

Are you ready to accept the gift of eternal life that Jesus is offering you right now? Let's review what this commitment involves:

- I acknowledge I am a sinner in need of a Savior—this is to repent or turn *away* from sin
- I believe in my heart that God raised Jesus from the dead—this is to trust that Jesus paid the full penalty for my sins
- I confess Jesus as my Lord and my God—this is to surrender control of my life to Jesus
- I receive Jesus as my Savior forever—this is to accept that God has done *for* me and *in* me what He promised

If it is your sincere desire to receive Jesus into your heart as your personal Lord and Savior, then talk to God from your heart

You are not born with God in your heart. Nobody can get you here… not your parents, spouse, church or friends. It is between you and God. Yes, our parents, spouse, church, and friends can help us in this journey. If you really desire to have that inner peace and have never personally had that moment where you invited Jesus Christ into your heart, then…

If you need direction, here is a suggested prayer:

"Lord Jesus, I know that I am a sinner and I do not deserve eternal life. But, I believe You died and rose from the grave to make me a new creation and to prepare me to dwell in your presence forever. Jesus, come into my life, take control of my life, forgive my sins and save me. I am now placing my trust in You alone for my salvation and I accept your free gift of eternal life."

For more information or reading material, call 1-800-A-FAMILY (232-6459). Then tell somebody about your decision that will forever change your life and give you a one-way ticket to eternal paradise, Heaven. You can know without a shadow of doubt where you will spend eternity. It has absolutely nothing to do with what religion you are. It's all about your relationship with Jesus Christ.

Made in the USA
Lexington, KY
13 November 2019

56920869R00102